HEARTLEADER

A TRAUMA-RESPONSIVE APPROACH TO TEACHING, LEADING, AND BUILDING COMMUNITIES

MATTHEW J. BOWERMAN

HEARTLEADER

© 2024 by TeacherGoals Publishing, LLC

All rights reserved. No part of this publication may be reproduced in any form or by any means—electronic, photocopying, recording, or mechanical means, including information storage and retrieval systems without the permission in writing from the publisher, except by a reviewer who may quote brief passages in a review. For more information regarding permission, contact the publisher at publishing@teachergoals.com. For bulk purchases go to teachergoals.com/bulk.

Published by TeacherGoals Publishing, LLC, Beech Grove, IN
www.teachergoals.com

Cover Design by: Alaina Clark-Weinstein and Heather Brown
Interior Design by: Heather Brown
Edited by: Dr. John Wick, Ed.D.
Copy Edited by: Heather Brown

Library of Congress Control Number: 2023950157
Paperback ISBN: 978-1-959419-15-0

First Printing: January 2024

Contents

1	1) The Adventures of a Heartleader
17	2) What is a Heartleader?
31	3) Finding the Pulse
39	4) Empowering Students
55	5) Prioritizing Parents
82	6) Supporting School Staff
99	7) The Emotional Aperture
108	8) Pulsecheck
115	9) Heartache
149	10) The Ones Who Know
175	Epilogue
179	Acknowledgements
180	About the Author
181	References

Dedication

To Kristi: my compass–all of this is possible because of you--my love to you always, in all ways; to our six courageous, Heartleading children that we share--to each of you: Honor, Sawyer, Decker, Kayla, Greyson, and Lyra, I wish for your lives to always be filled with the knowledge of how much you are loved and valued; seek to carry a lovelight for all people.

To the reader:

I would like to share with you that the first chapter of this book contains depictions and discussion around physical and sexual abuse. Some readers may find the content disturbing; please feel free to skip pages 1-4.

If you have been the victim of physical or sexual abuse, please know it is not your fault, and that you are not alone in your story; there are many of us here for support, and there are resources in the back of this book on page 178 to provide additional love, guidance, and support. You will always deserve that.

Interested in learning more? Sign up for professional development and join the Facebook group!

As a dedicated professional in the educational field, you're invited to enrich your practice through exclusive professional development opportunities offered by TeacherGoals, inspired by the profound insights of Matthew J. Bowerman's *Heartleader*. Scan the provided QR code to access information about professional development that will guide you in fostering authentic relationships and integrating love into every aspect of your educational journey.

Unlock a vibrant community of like-minded educators by joining the Heartleader Facebook group. This dynamic space is designed for collaboration, support, and shared experiences as you navigate the challenges and triumphs of implementing the principles outlined in the book. The QR code provided effortlessly connects you to this supportive network, where you can engage with fellow educators, exchange ideas, and collectively strive for positive change in your educational community.

Efficiency meets empowerment: Scan the Resources QR code once, and access a treasure trove of resources. A single scan grants you access to a comprehensive suite of resources that will empower you to become a transformative force in your educational setting. Don't miss out—take the first step toward cultivating a heart-centered approach to education by unlocking the potential within *Heartleader*.

HEARTLEADER:

[noun]

1) A person who has built a compassionate, empathetic, authentic sense of themself in order to intentionally love, guide, and empower all aspects of a school community.

2) A person who believes that love in education is the first and most valuable lesson one can give or receive.

3) A person who seeks only to lead, live, and learn with love as their guiding syllabus.

A Heartleader, as both an educator and student, knows that their love is unconditional and that for each day spent in a school community, it is all about authentic relationships, all about authentic love.

<u>Words related to Heartleader:</u>
Heartleading, love, love leading, love leader, unconditional love, educator, teacher, bridge builder, lifelong learner, servant leader

1. The Adventures of a Heartleader

Origin Story

Everyone has one, and they all have to start somewhere. My story's not very linear; it feels more like oddly spliced-together frames of a filmstrip damaged by smoke and left in the attic for too long. It's hard for me to see it within a specific timeline, or remember large chunks, and then all at once, in an instant, I'm triggered and tossed right back into what feels like the beginning. I find my mind transported; time and space shift, and it is as if I am nine years old, wearing my favorite Spiderman Underoos at 2 o'clock in the morning.

I've always been an insomniac by trade, often third-person narrating much of my own adventures. My 9-year-old self was no different. I can hear my whisper-voice fogging the bathroom mirror as I begin another one of my adventures, "There's Matthew, climbing through the jungle to the top of the ancient city," as I pull myself to standing on the vanity, straddling the sink. My scarecrow-thin shoulders barely hold my blue, satin cape in place, but I disregard its precarious hold on my shoulders and toss it back heroically! I check my Zorro-style mask and stare at my reflection, reassuring the world and myself that this very morning, the bathroom and all the world would be safe!

I discovered that no matter where I adventured or how far I climbed, it was my destiny to have my heart, as well as my secret identity, constantly tested time and again.

I close my eyes, and I'm brought back to visions of my fourth-grade teacher taking me… again… to that utility closet in the back of the classroom. I can smell French dressing on her breath. "Stop crying, and stop lying. You're acting like a spaz," she whispers, right before her left hand darts out, slapping me in the mouth. Her wedding ring clinks hard against my baby teeth sending shockwaves of physical and emotional turmoil that reverberate throughout my body, heart, and mind.

Later, alone and crying in a bathroom stall, I would do my best "Bruce Lee Chop" at the stainless steel toilet paper dispenser until my hand bled and blame it on a playground soccer accident. I chewed through my nails, biting them down to the quick, and still… unable to stop crying… I wet myself. I found myself standing again in front of another mirror that day, sweaty and awkward. I dumped water on my pants to hide the crime, pretending I had turned the sink handle too fast, but I couldn't hide from the smell or the taunts of 'Spazboy' that followed.

My origin story stumbles on, propelling me now in a rollercoaster-like fashion through hospital observation rooms and taking Ritalin at three years old until the shifting images jarringly halt the coaster. I find myself transported to my closet at fourteen years of age, sitting cross-legged inside a television box surrounded by comic books and Star Wars figures. I'm thumbsucking with fingernails again bitten down so far that they bled and hummed with pain at night.

No matter what I did, what costume or identity I tried on, I just couldn't get around or get away from all the BIG feelings, the BIG fears, and the BIG guilt tumbling around inside me. I was deep down in a hole, a long-forgotten well in a vast forest where light couldn't reach. The walls of the hole pressed in on me with its stone sides rubbing and cutting away at my innocence; the longer I was stuck there, the easier it became for the men visiting, dressed as angels, to hide monster faces while they fed. I mistook manipulation for kindness, violation for connection, attachment for love, and that hole swelled and selfishly took pieces from me.

I danced between allowing and struggling to push away the priests at school for years: sitting on that couch in the clergy house, reaching to rub my thigh, touching me down there with his hand in my 5th-grade lap, fingers searching; later a coarse, stubbled mouth against my small lips in the back of the sacristy while he silently prayed over me, tummy and hips pushing, pressing against me.

The hole grew, stretching down, pushing me under further, and the stories locked themselves away. I stacked my emotions and true self on shelves behind a paper-thin version of me that people could deal with. Still, people labeled me a 'spaz.' Some regarded me as an average child with average to low-average intelligence who was highly emotional with temper tantrums and meltdowns, who showed promise in the arts. I shoved back sleep, an eleven-year-old insomniac, so other monsters wouldn't find me there. I was manically rearranging bedroom furniture and rehanging posters throughout the night, rocking and pulling pieces of my hair out. Then, during the day, I would rage, hoping this creature called school and what happened in that principal's office so many times with her paddle and vulture-like hands, folding me over and taking down my Underoos, might keep a distance. Parts of me crumbled and died then, and parts of me held on, learning to fight along the way, to reclaim what had been taken.

Meeting Yourself Where You Are

We are connected - each of us, you, me, a person on the other side of the planet. Every human contributes to another's story.

Can you see any of yourself in my story or me in yours? For all we've lost and all we've gained, finding connections in stories is really powerful.

I bet that we are connected in ways we didn't even realize, and from that place, we have the opportunity to breathe into this work together and embrace our growth by sharing our stories.

You don't have to write profoundly poetic thoughts, wake up with magical powers, pull a sword from a stone, or sit down at an instrument and suddenly play Rachmaninoff in order to have value and a story as a human being. Many people's everyday origin stories are filled with herculean tasks of their own—great voyages, profound moments of doubt, miracles that defy description, insurmountable challenges, moments of glory, monsters both seen and unseen, and not nearly enough words in the dictionary to frame it all.

Children are draped in an origin story, and my story is not any different from that of thousands of other children. A tremendous amount of that storytelling, that origin-work, happens during childhood. It often happens not with the children as the tellers but *to* children, *at* children, most often without their requests or approval. They become the leading players and often its victims. In school, they come face-to-face with the majority of their primary socialization experiences featuring hosts of intentional and unintentional triggers as well as hundreds of adults who were also once children with their own origins. These adults entered a profession where they find themselves working to help children, and sometimes ending up, in their own misplaced pain, shattering them.

> Reflect on yourself and isolate a specific moment that has impacted your life and shaped who you've become. What is your moment?

Mementos From Traumatic Travels

What have you picked up, intentionally or unintentionally, and collected along the way as artifacts in the story of coming to terms with your own adulthood?

The body does not forget trauma; that is part of the lived experience. The information transferred from that experience may be visual, tactile, or emotional, but it moves into and through the body, affecting all of its critical support systems.

A traumatic experience may occur to the person where they become the target, in front of the person where they become its witness, or adjacent to the trauma where they experience indirect, collateral impact. It is important to note that regardless of the type of experience, an imprint is left.

Van der Kolk (2015) would go on to explain that trauma creates uncertainty in people and a sense of paralysis that finds them often disengaging from the world while also seemingly unable to not be emotionally affected by it. "Traumatized people chronically feel unsafe inside their bodies" (p. 98).

Trauma lives deep in bodies but so does love. Love leads us to this work and anchors our purpose in wanting to make that difference, to give back, to build, to even inspire if we're lucky. Families, students, and school staff all bring stories to the schoolhouse, and many of them are impacted by trauma in one form or another. Everyone brings their stories of school and what it meant to them or to their families at one point or another. A large part of the work of Heartleading asks us to hold these truths close, to recognize the grounding and healing power of love in all of its forms, and honor the stories of those who come before us each day. Heartleading asks us to consider this guiding question when moving forward with the work of safeguarding origins, building trust, and moving to coalesce relationships. In what ways can we operationalize love to support the social-emotional needs of students, families, and staff and mitigate the trauma that is brought into school communities daily?

> What are three ways you use love in your role to support students, staff, and/or families?

Putting Supports in Place

Trauma-responsive supports and the need for comprehensive social-emotional intervention in schools are such that they have become a significant part of the public health crisis. If there is anything the past several years have exposed for us is that people are incredibly resilient, but they are not okay, and a general weariness has occupied not only people's brains but their bodies and emotional lives as well.

What does support mean? What does it look like and feel like in your role?

The work of the Compassion Prison Project website elevates these needs with national Adverse Childhood Experiences (ACE) trauma data.

Figure 1

Adverse Childhood Experiences Trauma Data

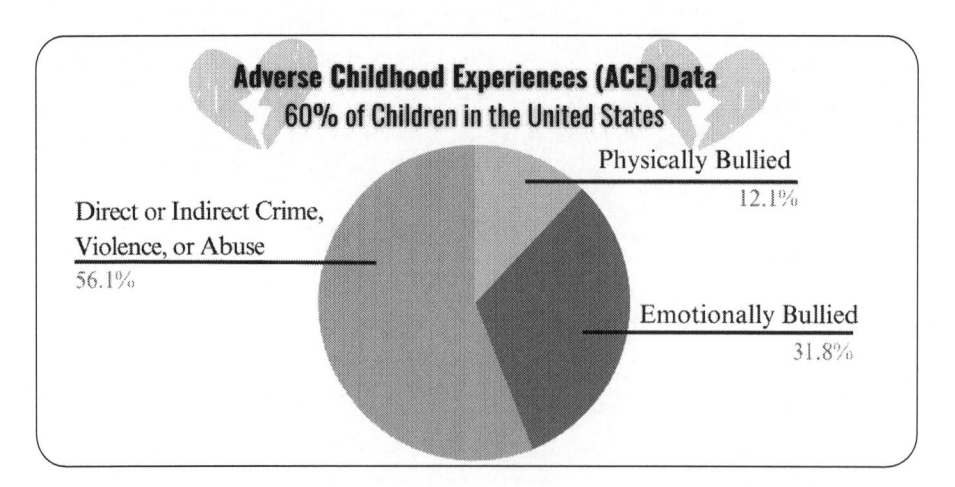

Adverse Childhood Experiences (ACE) Data
60% of Children in the United States

- Direct or Indirect Crime, Violence, or Abuse: 56.1%
- Physically Bullied: 12.1%
- Emotionally Bullied: 31.8%

Those statistics are playing out across this country even as I share these words. Yes, it is vital to reflect on data that is related to this graph in your own community and the success of your school community, but in what ways can you be responsive now that so much has happened? Typically, we would like our social-emotional support work to be preventative, but much of where we are feels reactive. How do you address what is constantly shifting and adapting? You must lean in, knowing that while all of this is fluid, schools will always have needs. Students, staff, and families will always need answers and support. That will not change, and therein lies your opportunity. In defining success measures at any level in school, it is imperative that one first considers how to build the healthiest, most well-informed, and consistently trained stakeholder community around trauma and social-emotional competency.

When you think about your school community as it relates to trauma-responsive training, social-emotional supports, and explicit communication about this work between stakeholders, ask these questions to ignite action and collaboration with your colleagues, students, and families:

- What does our data story state (not suggest) about your school within the three areas above?

- How are trauma-sensitive spaces identified in your community, and in what ways are they discussed and created to support school staff and students?

- What operational supports exist to safeguard and de-escalate students in crisis or with social-emotional needs? What types of communication are provided to the community around this type of work? Have external mental health partners been engaged, and if so, in what ways?

- What does the baseline data suggest for the school, and what impact data will be taken? How will it be used to redefine current and future protocols and practices around these three areas?

- How can the social-emotional or trauma-informed needs of your staff and student body be met while maintaining both a safe culture and climate and a place where learning remains as uninterrupted as possible?

Trauma and the Numbers

There are more than 332 million people living in the United States. According to the United States Census Bureau (2020), children under 18 make up approximately 78% of each U.S. state's population which is approximately 259 million people under the age of 18. Based on this 2020 census data, this suggests on average that 155,400,000 children under the age of 18 have been directly or indirectly exposed to abuse and/or criminal violence. That U.S. census data is considered outdated now; our population has increased, and with that, the number of children living with trauma.

Children from all types of experiences come to school every day to be curious, learn, play, make friends, and feel safe. Yet 155,400,000 of those children who are with us for seven to eight hours per day, are experiencing significant amounts of trauma and need safety and support (U.S. Census Bureau, 2020). That is a staggering amount of lives in the balance, but the opportunity before school staff is that they are "uniquely placed to observe variations in behavior and mood, making them a vital part of early identification and intervention" (Maclean & Law, 2022, Section 1, para. 7).

Just as the body can exist with trauma circulating through it, sometimes dormant and sometimes awake, it also draws it deeper beyond muscles and organs to a molecular level, as well as into the psyche–the spirit or soul of a person. It does not easily forget what it has experienced, and the emotional memories created leave clues behind. Like our fingerprints, the impressions remain.

It is the same way with the physical, emotional, and physiological feelings connected with how powerful love is. It imprints on the physical body and affects all the body's systems, weaving its way through memory and the senses. It pushes deep into the molecular fiber of a person, creating ripples felt at every level. From a neurological standpoint, there are chemicals like cortisol, serotonin, oxytocin, and dopamine released (Schwarz & Olds, 2015) into the body and the brain. Through love, it can begin a process of healing, learning, and rebuilding those areas.

Operationalizing love as a trauma-responsive and/or social-emotional set of tools could help to intervene and po-

"Love takes off masks that we fear we cannot live without and know we cannot live within."
~James Baldwin

tentially rebuild where some form of harm has created damage to any number of the external and/or internal parts of a person. Additionally, Dr. Richard Schwartz has pioneered Internal Family Systems (IFS), focusing on the understanding and healing processes of the multiple parts of our personality. In isolation or as a part of our collective systems, we must work to create balance and an "unburdening" of ourselves by working to identify what our parts might need. Schwarz's approach examines parts that resonate with shame, damage, or blockage, for example, and what we may need to heal those parts to reconnect them to our whole self and bring them back online, functioning and healing, within our collective systems. "When you can love all your parts, you can love all people" (Schwarz, 2022, p.186).

Dr. Richard Perry's research into trauma and healing led to a revisioning of a question about the ability of a person to recover and adapt from traumatic experiences; moving from "What's wrong with you?" to "What happened to you?" (Perry, 2021, p.29). This resonates with me, reminding me of how I became a teacher despite my origin. I know through my own personal work that I have used that question now to reframe my thoughts, my healing work, and my responses. That question, "What happened to you?" is one that reminds us that those origins, the initial storytelling, are not written by children, but often done *to* them, and *at* them.

Heartwork

Consider this homework for your heart–Heartwork–it extends to everything we do, and it is not easy. Heartleaders are called to do more in daily service because children, families, school staff deserve that level of preventative, responsive empowerment and care. It puts you in close contact with deeply personal needs, windows into people's lives that require everything from confidentiality to authentic listening around, at times, very challenging subjects. When negotiating any of this, it often places you in a trauma-adjacent position, where you are side-by-side with those experiencing immediate crisis, trauma, or sweeping social-emotional needs. The Heartwork being done to safeguard and nurture you is as much about your success and safety as it is about theirs. We see the numbers, we see the statistics, and meeting others where they are means knowing exactly where we stand.

> Is there something you would share with yourself about what happened to you along the way that led you here?

We must challenge ourselves to read between the lines of each of our stakeholder's stories, listen to their voices, and learn about all they have to offer. This work of storybuilding between the school and community makes intentions visible for prioritizing the emotional lives of children, creates an alliance anchored in developing trust, and establishes a belief in the success of the whole child. I find Pablo Freire's words grounding to this point in that "love is an act of courage, not of fear, love is commitment to others…the act of love is commitment to their cause—the cause of liberation" (Friere, 1970, p.89).

> Why do you do this work? What does it do for you?

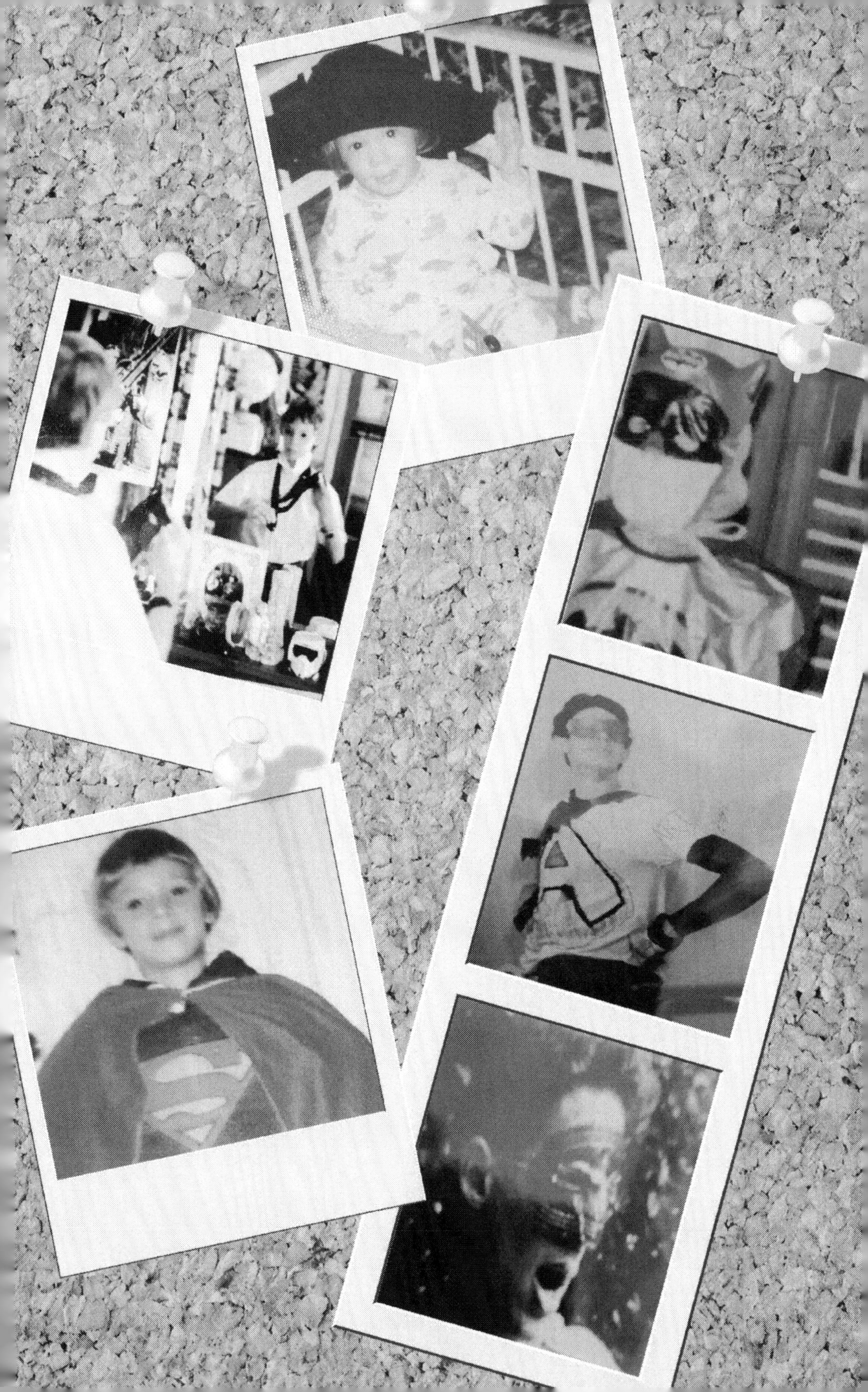

Try this. Paste an image here for yourself that paints part of the story of you. You are welcome to share them with me in the Heartleader Group on Facebook! I shared a few of mine on the previous page.

Facebook Group

2. What is a Heartleader?

One who has built a compassionate, empathetic, authentic sense of themself in order to intentionally love, guide, and empower all aspects of the school community; it's all about authentic relationships, all about authentic love.

Giving Permission

Heartleading is an ever-evolving process, and it becomes more nuanced the more personal it gets. I've shared the definition with you, but because we are examining roles across the entire spectrum of a school community, everyone engages in this work in different ways, and by extension, feels it differently too.

Everyone will come to this book, its stories, and its tools in different places in their careers and respective roles. Practice doesn't make perfect; practice makes permanent. We are looking to do just that, make permanent and sustainable shifts in our mindsets, behaviors, and responses as Heartleaders.

I'm learning to give myself permission to understand that I am not always as loving to myself and others as I could be. I'm learning that the world in which we are teaching and raising children feels much heavier and more alert than it did when I was a child. I build from my beginnings, recognizing in myself both privilege and imperfection as an administrator, educator, and member of a school system. I am learning to make decisions that operationalize love and learning on a high-stakes level that focuses on the teachable times we are in.

As I explore relationships and the dynamics of race and culture in my work, I learn to build my cultural competency and build out my knowledge of the people I safeguard as part of the community. I seek guidance from others and insights into the nature of both equity and education that is culturally responsive. My work within a school system is by extension the work and love of the community I serve.

In this way, I am more apt to be taught than to teach. While I have a front-facing role, I take intentional action to turn the mic over to the voices that need to be heard consistently and pursue sustainable equity action with other staff, leaders, and community members to lead change from change from our school improvement work on the ground. As Saffir and Dugan (2021) challenge, "White leaders must be careful of their approach to leadership and see much of their work as uplifting the voices of others, holding other white people accountable, and taking action in coalition with people of color" (p.89).

As I built my Heartleader approach, I learned that this quote further elevates the calling of Heartleading. We are called to stand in both love and solidarity for equity and inclusivity. These are big words, words of our times. We are in the business of human beings, elevating their safety, their rights, their futures, right? To that point, we must do all we can in our roles to engage and sustain students and families who represent every race, religion, sexual orientation, and culture. This ranges from hiring practices and professional development to those PTA nights and informal chats around the schoolhouse. Heartleading, then, is not a light-switch approach. It is lights full on, and it is imperative our love and learning are matched with a commitment to equity work, including being a part of dismantling and rebuilding.

I've been afraid, many times, in the early phases of my education career of making the wrong decisions in this work, of not making things clear enough in my approach, and of leaning away from the discomfort that comes from authentic engagement in this. I have learned that none of this operates in a vacuum, and I have sought out partners and learned to place myself in spaces that lean in. When you work to love in order to learn, you don't have any other choice but to lean in. You will make mistakes and face questions and confusion around not only yourself and your own biases but those around you. That is the right place to be because we are human and imperfect. That is not only our greatest unifying strength but our greatest vulnerability.

I cannot tell you how many times I have been in a classroom, in a meeting, or at a training where I kept asking myself and the universe, *tell me what you need from me, what is my purpose here, lead me forward in this work and I will be an instrument for it as it becomes clear–I just need direction and purpose.* Understanding your purpose is such a beautiful gift you can give yourself as an educator. How do you find it? How have you found it? It starts with questions around your values, your story, and the goals and priorities you have. There is a lot of discussion in education spaces and trainings about the why, finding and knowing the why in your life. I know it took me a great deal of time to ground myself in purpose where I wasn't drifting. I worked on questions like this when I first started teaching that led me to my why:

- Why has this opportunity found me now?
- Where were the moments when I stood in my own way, and why did that happen?
- Why does this matter to me?
- Why do I want to do this–working in a school community?
- Why do I want to serve?

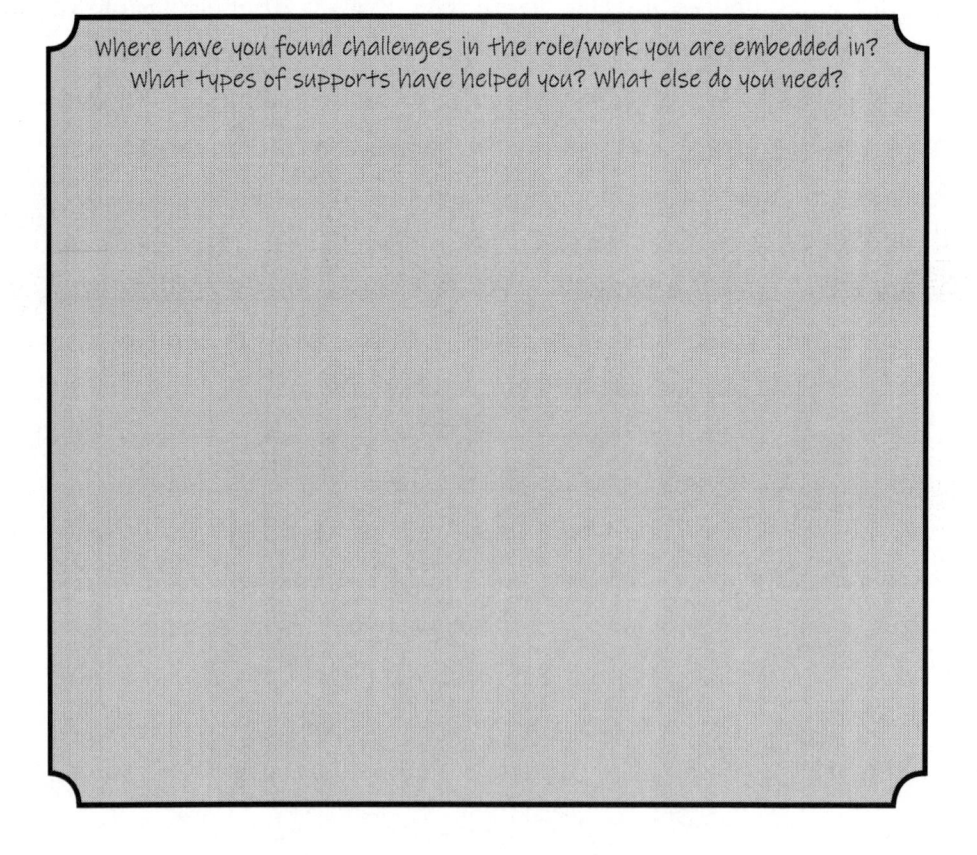

> Where have you found challenges in the role/work you are embedded in? What types of supports have helped you? What else do you need?

My understanding of education comes from having struggled through much of it, as well as learning to understand that my needs on an intellectual and emotional level were highly sensitive and distinctly different from others that I was exposed to. I was impacted by unresolved, and at times, recurring trauma as much as I was by my intellectual disabilities. To this day, much of how I love and learn is derived from those chapters of myself as well as the student and family stories that have filled my life with so much hope.

I still wrestle with the, "What happened to you?" question. Not because it is a label or a place to lay blame, but because it asks me to do work that is difficult. It asks me to be on alert for triggers, and consistently work to notice how my body feels to determine where I need to place my attention when supporting myself in the work I do with others. So I continue to prioritize my mental health as part of my Heartleading because why not? Much of that work has taught me about healing and forgiveness; key elements of skills we hope our K-12 and higher education students will understand and practice. It is hope in myself, hope in my family, hope in my recovery and healing, and hope in this educational profession that gives me what I need to rise every day and embrace what lies before me.

It is beautiful and messy, a mixed bag of that loving and learning process, but it's all mine. I am focused on loving myself to a better version of me and making me the most authentic husband, father, and Heartleader I can be.

> "Nothing ever goes away until it teaches us what we need to know."
> -Pema Chödrön

The Struggle Can Feel Beyond Real

There is nothing easy about all the things you, as an educator, navigate working with people and their origins, in building their capacities to be compassionate in their approaches and loving in their practices. Every person engaged in a school community has the opportunity to Heartlead. You do not need to know a student's trauma to love them, but you do need to get to know them in your role in school. Allen (2002) offers research to support the idea that young children who face personal challenges around trust, love, and attachment can struggle to identify and build healthy, positive social bonds as they get older. Children, by their nature, are social creatures who seek varying forms of socializing opportunities. One of the biggest struggles we saw, as a result of the pandemic, was that it stripped those socializing experiences away from children, and often left them in isolated spaces, to fend for themselves.

The majority of K-12 students existed in isolated states, almost like museum displays held behind velvet ropes, encased in glass, unable to connect or relate to people, places, and situations beyond their living environments. Students in fifth grade coming out of the pandemic, for example, had last been in a full year of school in third grade; challenges around maturity, attachment, school fatigue, and a limited understanding of positive, healthy socializing experiences made for many dysregulated behaviors. They struggled to make sense of the post-pandemic world in bigger bodies but were not intellectually or emotionally equipped to navigate that world.

Allen (2022) points out that unresolved issues in our lives can create blockages down the road. These early opportunities are where the school can take an active part. When school returned to in-person learning, much of those needs went unresolved. Without adequate supports, students had to find their own way back, resulting in a great deal of anxiety and feelings of loss. As a result, the literal school building and campus itself, as well as the adults present in it, became the primary source of triage, reconnection, healing, and education.

That is a lot of weight to carry; the struggle was beyond real! Educators in their own ways fumbled with this as well. The transition to online learning, then to hybrid, and then back to in-person created not only considerable compassion fatigue and uncertainty, but struggles with job performance, pressures to assimilate technology at a certain pace, and concerns around a lack of trauma-responsive training in the face of so many children's emotional needs. In addition, it cannot be overstated that adults, struggling to manage their own fears of illness, uncertainties around family safety and work, and the considerable pressures of coping with loss and traumatic changes, still have not completely found their way back to a full sense of normalcy years later.

Putting the Heart Into the Leading & the Heartleader's Action Plan

When you are Heartleading, where do you begin the work when there is so much before you in a (not-completely), post-pandemic world?

"Our schools cannot continue to exist or be treated as isolated entities in a community—those of us working with and in schools must support them to become more tightly connected to, in service of, and responsive to the communities in which they are located."
-Elena Aguilar

First, it is important to surround yourself with an equitable collective of people and skill sets who possess divergent thinking styles and adhere to the primary belief that *students come first*. Agreement on that is a fundamental necessity to be able to move forward with a Heartleader's mindset.

Second, the group should build a *Heartleading Action Plan (HAP)*. You can follow the subsequent steps in this order, or take them apart to design what your school community wants and needs.

> A plan only works with consensus from those you collaborate with and support. How would this plan, or one like it, serve your community? What do you need to make it happen?

Bridge-Building and Elevating the Heartwork

Heartleaders *bridge-build*. They construct opportunities to form connections, build trust, and by extension they begin to establish authentic, sustainable links between people, between school and home. Without the focus on bridge-building as a common practice grounded

Figure 2

Heartleading Action Plan

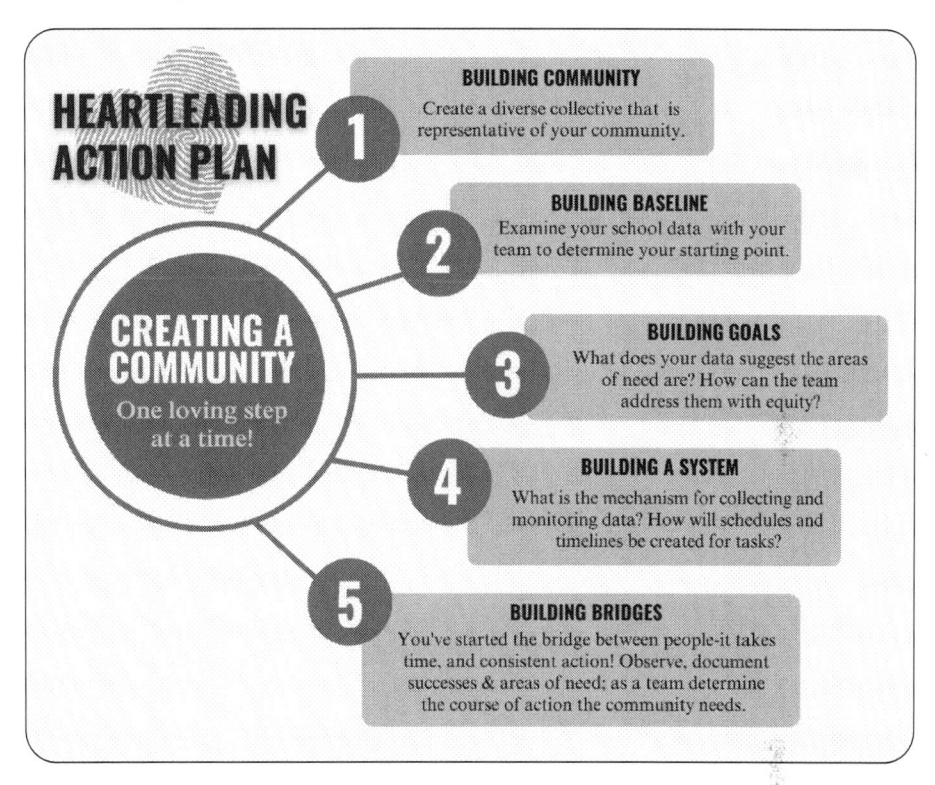

HEARTLEADING ACTION PLAN

CREATING A COMMUNITY
One loving step at a time!

1. **BUILDING COMMUNITY**
Create a diverse collective that is representative of your community.

2. **BUILDING BASELINE**
Examine your school data with your team to determine your starting point.

3. **BUILDING GOALS**
What does your data suggest the areas of need are? How can the team address them with equity?

4. **BUILDING A SYSTEM**
What is the mechanism for collecting and monitoring data? How will schedules and timelines be created for tasks?

5. **BUILDING BRIDGES**
You've started the bridge between people-it takes time, and consistent action! Observe, document successes & areas of need; as a team determine the course of action the community needs.

in culturally responsive action, access, and opportunity for students and families, both social-emotional health and instructional support will suffer exponentially.

You will need defined parameters. Without these, the relationships become blurred and will lack substance and long-term connectivity. Remember the relationships and the consistency with which they are constructed and maintained are at the heart of the matter. Swick (2003) examined the role of culture in the communication process and emphasized cultural differences as a means to strengthen relationships. Sharing information by empowering parents, caregivers, and guardians, dismantling barriers to cooperation, and recognizing parents' strengths and perspectives are fundamental to building strong relationships between the home and the school.

You must understand the people you serve, and this starts with learning about the community, its history, and the people who define it. You must be as transparent and reflective as possible with the reckonings and learning that come from engaging with so many communities and origins. I have always been told that beliefs are lived through action, and Heartleading prioritizes a culture of safety in developing relationships.

> A culturally safe environment is an environment which is safe for people: where there is no assault, challenge or denial of who they are, and what they need. It is about shared respect, shared meaning, shared knowledge and experience, or learning together with dignity, and truly listening (Williams, 2011, p. 213).

Communities must see you putting in the work to partner with them to develop the criteria for these culturally safe environments while you communicate your core values and make them visible in your actions. For example, collaborating with a community about how they prefer their communication–manner of delivery and frequency–is critical to building that framework of trust between partners. Schneider (2003) asserts parents depend on the information that teachers, school staff, and their administration provide, as well as how they shape an environment to promote safety and learning. They want to know their children will be safe and that they have spaces that are conducive to learning. Moving in this way with parents builds trust in your school community.

With the continued need for elevated levels of social-emotional response in school communities, national and international studies around relationship building, love in education, and love-based leadership have continued to evolve. Uusiautti & Määttä (2014), researchers at the University of Lapland in Finland, have been exploring love and its impact on behavior, wellness, and academics. Love can be seen as a virtue or strength representing human kindness, compassion, and affection. Their work states that the capacity to love can be found in every human being and therefore act as a skill that can be learned.

The work of educators focusing on the application of love-based approaches to teaching and leading must recognize that this work extends beyond the walls of a school and continues into neighborhoods, community partnerships, etc. Regular interactions between educators and parents have been proven, according to their research and others, to increase parent involvement in the school life of the student and in the parent-teacher relationship. This is to say that the bridge between school and home becomes not only more connected, but more affirming.

> The importance of effective relationships in building trust cannot be underestimated. Settings need to ensure that parents feel welcomed and valued as important partners in the educational process. Many parents have had negative experiences in schools themselves, and so the onus is on the setting to make sure this is minimized (Burnett & Thorsborne, 2015, p.160).

You can hold any role in a school and be a Heartleader –one does not need to have pain or trauma to be a Heartleader . It can just as easily come from a place of love for service, for supporting education and student wellness, or for being an advocate. It is critical to note that being a Heartleader is not taking on the role of the school counselor, school psychologist, behavior interventionist, social worker, or mental health provider-we have amazing people in our schools embedded in that work. Rather consider that it is a proactive, trauma-responsive lifestyle, an extension of your core values, operating authentically with a school community.

"Heartleading, yes, love gets us there. We need to understand one another more, and leaders need to be all about understanding those they work with. Empathy then is the road to compassion, and as a leader I have learned that there is more to understanding the feelings of another. It's about leveraging what the other is feeling and how I can go about helping to make them whole."

-Ann Hablangana, Delaware Dept. of Education, Associate of Educator Equity and Recruit; Educational Consultant

> Describe the relationship you have with families in your school community. What is working? What could be improved?

HEARTBEATS

Heartleading encompasses the following ideas:

- Applies a 'say and do' belief system, making sure they match in practice.
- Confronts bias and racism on a personal and systemwide basis; it is an equity-based approach, eliminating that which would marginalize and compromise the safety, academic and social-emotional lives of communities of color and indigenous communities.
- Educates instructional coaches to take all forms of data into account when building mechanisms to improve the academic and emotional lives of our students.
- Believes in the power of love to educate, to heal, to bridge gaps, and form true relationships.
- Moves from a place of love advocacy for the community they serve.
- Recognizes each story, complete with trauma, biases, privileges, and examines intentionally, in order to refine, disrupt, and correct practices.
- Empowers flexible thinking, capable of celebrating mistakes, and learning from finding various ways to love those they interact with.
- Love-lifts others in spite of differences in the way they are able to receive and seeks to share love as a way to create sustainable partnerships.
- Responds rather than reacts.
- Listens more than talks.

- Shows up in the community with families and meets them where they are.

I'm no longer just that boy in the origin story, although he is always with me. I've traded the cape for a three-piece suit and am tall enough to look into the mirror without climbing onto that sink. I'm still looking for the hero in myself on a daily basis. In my good and not-so-good days, I find that I'm able to even touch the edges of something *super* when I play alongside the children on the playground, listen to their stories, collaborate with staff on a problem of practice, or help a family get what they need.

I'm no longer the child who felt like he was in a hole, but I remember how dark it was. I carry the feeling of it with me, as well as the love that carried me away. Now, no matter what time it is, I am positive there's a world of schools for all of us to not only save, but to lead in love.

> What has shaped the way you love and the way you understand love? What is something you've read here that resonates with you?

3. Finding the Pulse

"You not only have to love the work [of teaching, leading, and educational advocacy], but you have to love the idea that you can build adult capacity in service of students and families. The questions you ask, how you resolve conflict, how you deliver difficult news, how you celebrate, mourn, sympathize, and support are all characterized by love for the work, and for the people in your charge."

-Dr. Sarah Sirgo, Chief of Staff, Frederick County Public Schools, Maryland; Author, speaker, trainer

Taking the Pulse as a Heartleader

Heartleading places an educator on the frontlines of care and support for every aspect of a school community; *for all those in your charge,* and *it's an unbelievable amount of responsibility.*

Taking the pulse asks us to be able to be present, to plug into the community, and to be a part of its flow, its movement, and to adapt to its dynamics. Taking the pulse places you into the life of school where you become aware of more than just the space you may occupy, extending your awareness and intention past those walls. Pulse checking is a skill to be developed, felt, perceived, and sensed with a high degree of awareness. You will experience success and disaster, and there are miracles and grief. You may have already felt tremors like that in your work and life from being so hyper-tuned into virtual school life during Covid… talk about trying to find a steady pulse! There are things you have each seen and felt, events that defy all human description, but they stick with you, making you question yourself, your decisions, and your profession.

I know I have been in that place many times in twenty-six years. I think it's okay to have those questions; for me, they help to reignite my why, my purpose for what I am doing, and who I am doing it for. There are also conversations with students that renew your faith in all things precious and wonderful. There are those long, sleepless nights, with the faces of students and parents running through the movie in your mind, and there are moments when someone thanks you for what you do. It fills your heart, and lets you know that what you do matters. None of this has ever felt easy to me, not in the least. I wonder if you feel, or have felt, that way at some point in your career? As I have it before, this is personal work, and that keeps it emotional as well. There are all kinds of risks associated with interacting around emotions and people in vulnerable places.

The Things We Carry, The Things We Need

What would make your work easier? What do you need less of? How could you optimize your responsibilities, and thereby increase your impact?

At times, the things we carry feel like it's all too much. The pressures of both the academic and social-emotional needs of students, the meetings and testing, navigating constantly changing technologies, planning, grading, and trying to carve out something for yourself along the way...sometimes we carry far, far too much. I am reminded in those moments, when it all piles up, how important it is to put things down. This becomes especially important when you are working in conditions that may feel highly emotional, and you are asked to engage in work with peers, students, or community members that you may not have the capacity or training for.

Sometimes, the important things we require can get lost in the busyness of school. To address this, setting aside specific time and space for staff to express their needs and preferences can greatly contribute to the development of a strong Heartleading mindset. Educators' needs are different across roles, grades, and types of educational settings, but those needs must be prioritized, and staff must be provisioned with the time, tools, and opportunities to design their successful pathway.

Maclean & Law (2022) examined educator roles by interviewing teachers and studying a variety of influences that shape the school day as well as the hours beyond to gather feedback about what educators needed to be able to approach their roles more effectively. The feedback was overwhelmingly attached to a lack of knowledge and training from teacher training programs and job onboarding to continued professional development throughout the school year. This lack of training may be one of the determining factors that impede an educator's willingness or ability to be able to engage with students around their social-emotional support and/or trauma.

When staff see a student in crisis or a visible struggle taking place in the classroom, they may choose to avoid the engaging conversation because they feel they don't have the training or tools to be able to productively respond and de-escalate a situation, not because they don't want to help.

A promising way to break this stress cycle is by preparing teachers to manage behavioral challenges in the classroom, which is associated with higher self-efficacy and lower burnout (Pas, Bradshaw, & Hershfeldt, 2012 as referenced in Kim et. al). The findings signify the importance of providing teachers with proactive classroom management strategies to enable them to create an orderly learning environment and alleviate stress (Kim et. al, 2021).

> Does any of this sound familiar to your role? What training would help you do your job better with students? Do you know who to ask, or how to get it?

Mayday, Mayday! It's Another Day in School!

911, what is the nature of your emergency?

(I HAVE STUDENTS, STAFF, AND A COMMUNITY I AM TRYING TO HELP, AND I'M LOSING MY MIND!)

Are you somewhere safe?

(I'M NOT SURE. DO WE GO INTO A LOCKDOWN OR A MODIFIED SHELTER? ARE THERE HARD CORNERS IN THIS ROOM? MY PHONE'S AT 4%, WHO'S GOING TO COME ON THE PA? ARE 32 OF US REALLY GOING INTO MY SUPPLY CLOSET? I'M HAVING SOME TROUBLE BREATHING, AND MY HEART IS BEATING REALLY FAST.)

Is there someone there to help you?

(THIRTY-TWO FOURTH GRADERS ARE JUST LOOKING AT ME.)

Do you need an ambulance?

(I NEED FIFTEEN MORE GLUE STICKS. I'VE GOT FIVE. NO– HOLD ON, NOW I'VE GOT SEVEN BROKEN CHROMEBOOKS. I NEED TO FINISH GRADING THEIR PERSONAL NARRATIVES. I HAVE TO PAY MY LATE WATER BILL. I NEED COFFEE, AND I THINK I MAY BE LATE FOR BUS DUTY!)

Stay where you are.

(AND I HAVEN'T GONE TO THE BATHROOM IN SIX HOURS!)

> A collection of school staff created that imaginary call over the past eleven years, based on what they've experienced — I'd love to know which part resonated with you the most. Scan the code to go to the Heartleader Facebook Group!

Prioritizing Heartleading in Three Steps

Taking a pulse, knowing where to find it on the body, and how to accurately take it requires training. It can be the difference between life and death. I think this is where educators' feelings lie around pride in their calling and their role in education. It is life on the line, and they want to be as ready, aware, and trained as possible to be able to respond and provide the right type of care and support. Over the course of the next three chapters, I will be sharing insights and strategies into the three core areas of Heartleading:

- Empowering students
- Prioritizing parents
- Supporting staff

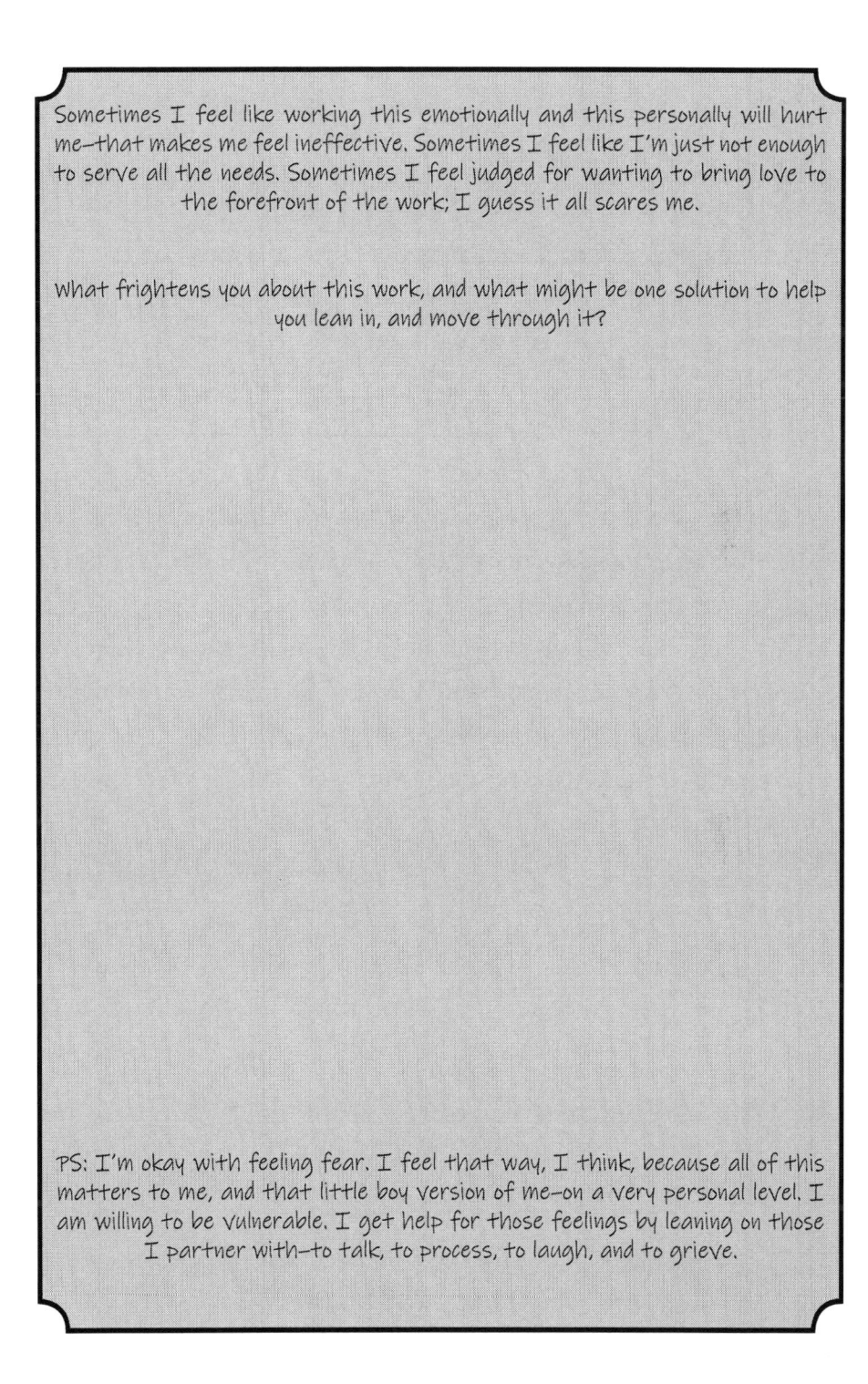

Sometimes I feel like working this emotionally and this personally will hurt me—that makes me feel ineffective. Sometimes I feel like I'm just not enough to serve all the needs. Sometimes I feel judged for wanting to bring love to the forefront of the work; I guess it all scares me.

What frightens you about this work, and what might be one solution to help you lean in, and move through it?

PS: I'm okay with feeling fear. I feel that way, I think, because all of this matters to me, and that little boy version of me—on a very personal level. I am willing to be vulnerable. I get help for those feelings by leaning on those I partner with—to talk, to process, to laugh, and to grieve.

HEARTBEATS

Heartleading places a staff member in the position of learning how to take the pulse of a school and then placing them directly into it. It also:

- Recognizes that staff are human beings with their own stories, traumas, and pain. While this gives them context to support, it does not make them trauma-responsive experts. They require training year-round in supports and strategies to navigate the complexities of students with trauma and social-emotional needs.
- Challenges you to ask yourself tough questions. What portions of your role are you uncomfortable in, and what are you doing for yourself, personally and professionally, to mitigate this?
- Gives you permission to be human–to be uncertain, to feel stress or fear in this role. When you give yourself permission to be human in the daily "mayday" of school life, what does that mean to you? How do you do this–giving permission to be human?

4. Empowering Students

"Relationships are the agents of change and the most powerful therapy is human love."

-Dr. Bruce Perry & Maria Szalavitz, *The Boy Who Was Raised as a Dog*

Empowering students means that you have created a life with them outside of textbooks, slideshows, and assessments. Without relationships, nothing else is possible. This is the critical tenet that must guide everything; without relationships, nothing else is possible. It is incumbent on school leaders and staff to make authentic investments in the community, prioritizing the value of the people, the importance of their voices, and consistent, culturally responsive messaging that lets each stakeholder know they belong.

The everyday experience of school then becomes active engagement in opening doors and securing paths; knowing that this foundational work is developing long-term trust and transparent communication again placing your most valuable asset, your people, at the forefront of every decision you make. Setting students on that path to claim their education is a gift we can give them by helping them in five key areas:

- Identifying their purposes for learning
- Engaging in conversations around the benefits of being both curious and pursuing some form of educational learning (e.g. school to higher education, school to military/fire/first responder/law enforcement, school to trade school)
- Creating the conditions for student-educator engagement by scaling out meaningful tasks to develop globally conscious, critical thinkers
- Providing opportunity and access to engage in scholarship, with academics, the arts, athletics, etc via multiple sources and opinions
- Challenging them to reflect on their humanity, their ability to demonstrate compassion and inclusivity, and how to shape a series of social and life skills/behaviors that prepare them for the world they are growing up in

These are by no means everything we can do when we empower our students. However, these five areas broadly work to direct them without coercion, to offer choice and options, and to probe their own lives and ideas with culturally responsive questions. Consider these training questions for yourself as you consider your role:

- In what ways have you and your school empowered students?
- How do students exercise agency in your school community?
- Can students see themselves in the opportunities, ideas, and conversations being presented by the adults they engage with?
- What do your students express about their school community?
- In what ways have you seen schools diminish students?
- What mechanisms (both processes and collection/monitoring tools)

have been designed and implemented in your school to provide a way to collect and address long-term student needs: both academic and social-emotional?

"We just want teachers and the people working in school to see us for who we are, to accept us for all the times we do right, and all the times when we mess it up, you know? We're not perfect, and school can be really hard, but it's good, like really good to know you can come to school and there is a teacher who has your back."
-Nakiya, 14

Empowering Places Students First

Students spend a great amount of time in school in addition to the approximately seven or so hours of instructional time. There are after school daycares, sports practices and games, music rehearsals, and clubs of every kind.

Let's make sure we remember there are also the many students, at various ages, who may just be out reading a book on the basketball court or walking along the back fence because school is safe to them and what waits for them away from school is something, or someone, they would rather avoid.

Heartleaders recognize that with all of this activity nourishing the pulse of a school, it is not about the hours a leader is in the building, but what they do with the time spent there. The time when students are involved in these activities and projects presents an incredible time for connection.

Often our students are in their zone, in their environment, shining, doing one or more of their favorite things, and you have stepped into their element. Fagell (2017) suggests that when you show interest in the lives of students and attend their games, plays, and concerts, they'll know you care. As a result, they'll be more invested not only in you and the relationship they have with you but in the learning process. These are those opportunities that can get missed or overlooked in the weight of grading, exhaustion from long work days, and meetings - all valid things - but there are so many opportunities that can be created to see your students do some of the very things that they will paint their futures with. Attending these events makes you seem more approachable and more real to them. Students may feel more comfortable approaching you for help. It's also a way to get to know students' families in an informal and unpressured setting.

When you create a pattern of seeing students in these places, it allows them to see you in a more humanized, less formal, way. You will be amazed at how relationships can positively shift to reflect these efforts, and the conversations that emerge are equally rewarding for what you can build with these students.

Here are a few of my treasures I'll share with you that have stuck with me over the years from things students have said or written to me about relationship-building that took place outside of my classroom:

"You came to be with me at my grandfather's funeral. My family and I never forgot that."
-Bobby, Gr. 11

"When I come to school in the morning, and see you outside, you make my day happy. You are my beautiful unicorn."
-Jacqueline, Gr. 1

"You were the only one who supported me coming out. You never judged me or singled me out. You just let me find my way: the dressing up, the makeup, all of it, and you let me know you were proud of me, and there for me if and when I needed you, and when I did need you, you were there to listen. You just let me find me."
-Ry, Gr. 12

"Every theatre performance, you wrote us notes. You made everyone feel special. You found a way to let everyone know what they were doing mattered. I still have those notes today."
-Katie, Gr. 8

If you haven't already, create a box, a folder, a special place to keep the notes and drawings, a place to go when you need that boost. You will get those treasures, and there will be times when you should revisit them. I hope you are thinking of some of your own students' words right now. How are they making you feel? I have an idea; use this area to place a few here in your book as you use this to reflect on your Heartleading. Remember, the *why* is as important as those notes students have given you across the years.

> What are a few things students have shared with you about your impact on them?

Educators must consider the impact in everything they do, just as children feel that impact in everything they are. A significant part of children's emotions is tied to how they perceive things and how adults treat them. When caring adults provide nurturing and affectionate experiences, it can strongly contribute to changing their negative self-beliefs (Craig, 2008). Relational traumas in their lives have taught them that they are only broken, only defective, and most likely unworthy of love. The things done to them and around them only reinforced those concepts; healthy adult relationships can reverse this. It takes time and a commitment to build those relationships, and school can be a safe space designed to support that.

During the time students are in school, there are tremendous opportunities for adults to teach the students adaptive skills and to become sources of support and love for them. That work is as rewarding as it is challenging, and it is work borne of patience and time. As I was considering this relational trauma in my personal journey, I was reminded of a story that has been embedded and kept alive in my memory:

I was twelve and in the seventh grade. I had just learned that there was a program in Maryland called the Maryland Summer Center for the Gifted and Talented in the Arts. I had been singing and performing from a very young age, and this was unlike anything I had ever heard of: a place for people like me, a place that might make me feel like I belonged somewhere.

Let me set the scene: I ran up to my computer teacher, Mrs. J, who was positioned at the portable door to my computer class. She was a very tall woman with a presence and energy to match. She was very intelligent and very partial to certain students; I was not one of them. It was clear from previous interactions that she felt I was too much to handle. The following conversation has influenced me and remained with me for much of my life. I look back upon it as if it were a brief scene from a play.

Enter young Matthew: gangly, awkward, breathless, flush with excitement, rushing to the door of his computer class. Mrs. J steps in front of Matthew as he approaches the door, stopping him in her shadow.

Matthew: Guess what?!

45

Mrs. J: You need to slow yourself, and settle down, what is it?

Matthew: I just got this information from the flier in the front office. There's this summer program for arts kids, who love theatre, singing, and you have to audition for it, and because I love to sing I am going to audition-

Mrs. J: You won't get into that, you have to be really good.

Matthew: I will get in!

Mrs. J: Those programs require a lot of hard work.

Matthew: I know I can get in!

Mrs. J: You shouldn't get your hopes up, or you'll be disappointed.

Matthew: What do you mean?!

Mrs. J: That's enough yelling now, that's enough..stop crying, come inside.

Matthew, torn in half like a badly written essay, melts into a seat in front of the enormous monitor, drops his floppy disc to the floor, and stares at the dull, green, cursor flashing in the black ocean of the screen.

END SCENE.

I have no other concrete recollections of that teacher, but I have never forgotten that moment and what it did to me, to an already bruised psyche. What she said, how she said it, how she made me feel. I remember feeling rage, crying, and telling my mother about what had happened. Knowing how much I loved the arts, my mother just gave it to me in the way she has always lived her life–unwilling to be stopped by anyone or anything. *"Matty J (yes, she calls me that) if you want this bad enough, she can't stop you. No one can stop you, but you. So she said that to you, so what? Do you really care about what she says? It doesn't matter because this is about you going after what's important to you, not what she thinks."*

Along with the time my childhood dog died, and my mom was with me when I buried the dog, this remains one of my best moments with my mother. Without directly telling me, I think she was always aware, as challenging and emotional as I could be, that I had always been a little different, more 'high strung' as she put it, more emotional, always daydreaming, and marched to my own drum. While this made me a target along the way, it also allowed me to stand out from the crowd.

I would follow her helpful advice, ignore that teacher, go on to audition, and be one of only a few males to be selected in 1987. I was accepted to attend for Choral Performance (singing), and I would go on to audition, and be selected for over ten consecutive years for the Choral Music/Musical Theatre Arts programs there. As I got older, I would go on to serve as a counselor and even a teacher being a part of the performance

"Careful the things you say, children will listen. Careful the things you do, children will see and learn. Children may not obey, but children will listen. Children will look to you, for which way to turn, to learn what to be. Careful before you say, 'Listen to me,' children will listen."
—Stephen Sondheim

education programming all the way up until the late 1990s. Despite all of that effort and joy, I have also carried the memory of that teacher and her impact throughout my life, and while I do not remember much else about her, I remember all of that afternoon at her door, what it took away, and what it left broken up inside of me.

This is my point; children remember, families remember.

The Empowering Mindset

All children can learn, and all children learn differently.

Heartleaders recognize that expectations for students across a school's landscape must be high and anchored in a flexible mindset. All children can learn and be met where they are to expose learning gaps and create strategies to design goals and measures for success. Each student brings incredible value to their community. From this work built with students, impact can be measured, and follow-up evidence can be collected to look at the type of impact you, as the Heartleader, has made.

Talking about mindset and impact, Hafen (2015) notes that students need structures and expectations to guide their work and that students tend to rise or fall to the level of expectations that their teachers have for them. If a teacher is inflexible, bound in bias, or has perceptions about what a student may or may not be capable of, this could create a self-fulfilling prophecy within the student. Students at any age can sense how a teacher feels about them and what a teacher thinks about them whether it is voiced out loud or not. Declines in student academic performance, self-esteem, self-concept, engagement, and student motivation could all be casualties of teachers, or school staff, who are unable or unwilling to be flexible and empowering in their mindset. This destructive spiral could then possibly further evoke negative expectations from the teacher.

In terms of sustainable, positive impact, as well as demonstrating a desire for authentic connections separate from the traditional classroom experience, a solid strategy involves collaborating with a family and showing up for students outside of school in spaces and places that matter to them because *children remember.*

Student Voice is the Student-Empowered Future

When we empower, it is true that we are creating a connection that can promote wellness and learning in ways that make school come to life for a student, but empowering them and using their voice to shape the decisions being made about their education and future outlasts the conventional time they are in school.

When you empower the voice of students, it is important to celebrate mistakes, risk, trial and error, and open discourse with equitable parameters to guide the interactions.

There are phenomenal examples of school systems and educational programs utilizing student voice at high levels in

"In and around schools, we routinely fail to share necessary and accurate information about who young people are, what they can do, what they need, and how they are doing."
-Mica Pollok, SchoolTalk: Rethinking what we say about-and-to students every day

both national and international spaces from Canada to the United Kingdom, Vermont to Cleveland.

Cook-Sather (2020) conducted research around elevating student voice with regard to engagement, improving school climate, and academic performance increase. They researched the Youth and Adults Transforming Schools Together (YATST) organization in Vermont created by Helen Beattie and now under the umbrella of UP for Learning. For over twelve years, students and secondary teachers have partnered to discuss what is and is not working in classrooms and what solutions can be created to enhance learning. Over 3,000 students have taken active leadership roles in at least one UP initiative. There are over 113 schools participating with more than 150 educators completing an UP graduate course.

Cleveland High School has facilitated a number of relationships and practices focused on student voice by training thousands of students and teachers and offering their YATST workshop called "A Motivational Lens on Transformative Youth-Adult Partnership Experiences" in Vermont to share some of its practices (Chopra, 2014). The focus within these programs is giving autonomy and leading to the students who work in conjunction with educators to determine the most efficient and engaging delivery systems. UP initiatives also focus on students working directly with school administration at round table meetings around educational protocols and policy as well as reforms that affect curriculum, testing, and other academic support.

The learning of the future is dependent on the empowerment of the student as a highly active leader and participant in a classroom experience that is anything but linear and traditional. A Heartleader embedded in these spaces must recognize that the relationship between student and teacher is interchangeable, fluid, and marked by a mutual patience, curiosity, and interest in discovery and reflection. Many of the future careers our students will embrace are built around technology, inventions, and ideas that haven't even created yet. Helping to build those globally conscious, critical thinkers will place us as the adults in situations that challenge what we know, or think we may know, especially about the merging of education, teaching, and technology. The subsequent student feedback won't always be in agreement with ours or even be in alignment with your core values or beliefs. However, it is vital to building a fully realized version of themselves and promoting their own sense of agency and accountability that they are heard, and that active, transparent work is done with the information they provide.

Here are the experiences of three very different students from different backgrounds with things they shared with me about being able to have their voices heard, acknowledged, and supported. Some of it was celebratory. Some of it was very messy, but it was their voice, and our shared experience. It created a lasting impression for us both.

"It didn't matter how many times I told you, you still listened, and you let me know you would keep listening until I was over it or didn't need to talk about it anymore. You told me it wasn't my fault and let me know I wasn't going to be alone when I

> "By sharing power with students, by listening to them and seeking to follow their advice, we have learned that educators, researchers, and policy makers are more likely to promote contexts through which the voiceless have voice, the powerless have power and from such spaces hope can emerge."
> -Pablo Friere

worked through it."
-Kara, Gr.11

"We asked if we could design the lesson, put together the project in groups as a class, and grade it with you. When you said yes I was like, really? Suddenly we got to take control of what we were going to learn and how. It was really cool. I still remember it."
-Armand, Gr .7

"I told you I did Tae Kwon Do, and you said you did too. It was my belt test, and I looked up, and you were at the door. You said you'd come, but I couldn't believe it! You were really there and you remembered. It meant alot to me that you were there."
-Trey, Gr. 5

Coordinating efforts to empower student voices around school improvement requires creating tools and/or mechanisms to build time into class schedules, town halls, or master calendars in order to connect with students and collect their feedback. Most importantly, it also requires time with equitable groups of the student body to build the questions, based on what you want to know.

Consider these initial guidelines as you put student voice surveys into effect:

- Identify your baseline data during the first month of school; utilize your district's learning management system (LMS) to archive this feedback in order to examine it.
- Let students and families know it is coming, and determine methods

of communication and languages to share it in.
- Keep it specific but simple. 3-6 questions.
- Create opportunities to process information with students after staff have met and reviewed the information.
- Create follow-up opportunities with the student and family community after staff have designed responses to the students to share the considerations and/or changes.
- Make sure that if you are collecting voice data you have an intentional plan in place to use it to shape future work in your school and community.
- Incorporate a mid-year and end-of-year version to gauge feedback around how the student experience has evolved or devolved.

Please enjoy the FREE Heartleading Tools of Service by scanning the QR code. Each of the book's resources is archived here beginning with the tool for capturing student voice for elementary, middle, and high school, so you only need to scan it once. If you are in higher education and would like a similar resource for orientation, surveys, email me at: heartleaderlove@gmail.com, and we can discuss your college or university's needs!

HEARTBEATS

Heartleaders step forward into each day knowing:

- Kids come first every day.
- Relationships are the determining factor with children above all else.
- Every child's story should be valued and honored.
- Real knows real. Be authentically you. They can tell if you're not.
- Empower students to become the architects of their lives and success.
- Children have amazing skills, insights, and knowledge to share. Listen and pay attention.
- Connections with students cannot be developed where control and/or compliance are pursued as the norm in learning spaces.
- Children will remember how you treat them and how you make them feel.
- Model in your own behavior what you hope to see in your students.

5. Prioritizing Parents

Parenting Power

Parents and families come to us with their own stories and perceptions of school. They have their own voice that needs to be heard and can be tremendous advocates for their students as well as the broader work of the school. They engage in a myriad of ways, but they are out there. Prioritizing them asks us to determine the ways we will bring them from outside to inside the building and how we can create cohesion and support. To work with families, you must first learn to understand them. Consider these guiding questions when collaborating with your parents and families.

- How are parents/families critical to the success of your school?
- What do your parents express about the school community you serve?
- How is their voice represented in your school?
- In what ways are parents utilized in your school community?
- Do staff have the time and space to identify, reflect, and dismantle biases held against parents/families in your community? What is the lens, the approach by which they do this (e.g. Culturally Responsive, Anti-Racism, etc.)?

Parent Perspectives

We have their children in our care for seven or more hours per day. We are, by doctrine of 'in loco parentis,' their stewards when they are not in the care of their parents/caregivers. The doctrine of 'in loco parentis' is Latin for "in the place of a parent," and helps, I think, to anchor our purpose in education. We safeguard and provide the space, relationships, communication, and connection that are conducive to learning and wellness.

Years ago, as new administrators, a colleague of mine was talking about working with parents and their needing to understand the weight of the demands on school leaders. I agreed with his view on the weight of the responsibility leaders bear, but I also pointed out the fear and uncertainty of sending one's child/children out into a place where they are not explicitly certain of what goes on. That can weigh heavy on a parent or caregiver; as a parent I frequently feel it too. Additionally, social media and the neverending news cyles reporting school violence and the turbulent global climate have families and caregivers anxious and wondering just what impact these issues will have on their children, and what long-term harm will come from it all.

To that end, by the nature of our role, parents look to place their trust in us. They want to believe that we can bring their child home safely each day, and help them learn to read, write, and make good decisions. They want to be involved in the ways they can, and they want more than anything for their children to learn and thrive. Tudor (2022) promotes the belief that when school staff reinforce positive, interactive relationships with parents and make it known from the beginning that they are partners in the school life of the child and the community, interest, inspiration, and involvement increase.

Interviewing Parent Teacher Association (PTA), Parent Teacher Organization (PTO), and Parent-Teacher-Student-Association (PTSA) members over the years has provided many insights into what is helpful for school staff to consider when first building associations and trust between teachers and parents.

- Do you know my child's name?
- What else do you actually know about my child?
- When you call–what is the purpose of the call, and how are you approaching that conversation? How have you prepared for a call with me (e.g. is an interpreter needed, do you need caption services for deaf/hard-of-hearing parents, is there a cultural greeting that is appropriate to acknowledge, are you calling at a time that is appropriate for a conversation)?
- If the call is a challenging call around behavior or areas of academic need, can you frame the call around positives for my child as well? What does my child do well?
- Depending on what the call is about (e.g. failing grade) is this the first time you are making contact about the grade, and if so, why is this the first time I am hearing about it? When did you know about the grade/concern?
- How far are you willing to go to hear me as the parent and support my concerns?
- Will you keep your word or the things you say you will do to support us?
- How's your follow-up and follow-through with regard to my child?

In twenty-six years of education, one of the biggest pieces of advice I have gotten from families is that they just want to be heard. They want to make sure that a school has *really heard* them and not just listened.

They want to know the school can be responsive in ways that meet the needs of their child. They want to be kept in the loop and a part of the loop around any decision-making for their child (e.g. disciplinary consequences, setting up an Educational Management Team meeting, moving a child into an academic intervention).

Communication is one of the most critical elements of school improvement critiqued by parents in school systems across the country, and "every communication exchange, regardless of format, should reflect a thoughtful, planned approach and should be viewed as an opportunity for teachers to promote parent partnerships and, ultimately, to support student learning" (Graham Clay, 2005, p. 126).

School for educators never seems to operate just within those daylight hours. Much of the critical trust work between families and school staff happens across random and varied circumstances such as:

- The first time you meet at Kindergarten orientation
- Car rider line
- The grocery store
- Back to School Night
- 6:30 pm Friday phone call about something that happened to their child
- Signing out their child for a dentist appointment
- Spring musical
- Sharing their culture during International Night
- Individualized Education Plan (IEP) meeting
- An issue involving their child's behavior at recess

Prioritizing parents simply means that when parents/caregivers come to you with questions, concerns, and/or needs, remember what you would want in terms of communication, attitude, and tone if it were your own child or family member. Poor communication can only seek to undermine any positive work you do and compromise both goodwill and a parent's belief that you have the best interest of their child in mind.

Let's also be pragmatic. As an educator, it can prove challenging to navigate various issues with parents, and sometimes it can be downright messy. Working to emphasize the parent-educator relationship as a partnership, Heartleading makes the following beliefs transparent:

- Parents have tremendous knowledge and skills they can bring to the table.
- They want to know their children are safe and treated equitably.
- They want to be heard; they have stories that need to be heard.
- When it comes to their children, they want to know what you knew, when you knew, and what you did about it.
- They want to know that administration is fair and responsive.
- They want you to follow up with timely correspondence.

Having a parent-teacher conference, at any grade level, can be anxiety-producing for parents and educators. For any number of reasons, most adults remember these conference events from their own childhoods, and invariably an unpleasant memory surfaces. Let's try flipping the script on those painful memories and overall perceptions of meeting with the teacher.

> Try out these five strategies for establishing an effective communication routine with families around student progress meetings of any type—email me and let me know what works, as well as any other strategies we can share in our Facebook Heartleading community!
>
> Facebook Group

Establishing Routines for Parent-Family Communication

1. Gathering

Create an event when the year starts, a potluck of sorts, where families gather. You share a meal together and discuss parent feedback around effective conferences. Build that out into a resource, a shared, living document where all of that feedback is shared. Take photos of your event and share them out with your families.

2. Spreading the Word

Apart from the schoolwide communication, how are your parents able to sign up for a time, and are there options for in-person and virtual? Would you consider a home visit conference or a meet-up at their neighborhood playground if they have childcare issues? As you learn about them, what do your parents need?

3. Setting the Tone

When it's time, welcome them in with words and visual messaging that celebrates their entrance to your space; consider sharing a collage of those photos from the event in your space.

4. Seating and Proximity

Are you seated with the parents at a square or rectangular table? Place yourself near or alongside, but don't set yourself opposite to them, or far away. You can't show them the comparison growth samples in their child's writing or review their mathematical thinking on an algebra problem seated far away. You are seeking some form of connective proximity and a willingness to not be afraid of them but inspired by them and excited to be present in this 10-15 minute conversation about their child. In elementary classrooms, have seating that is appropriate for adults. Each grade level will require something different from your space and approach.

5. The Heart of the Meeting

Chunk the meeting into parts, and focus the meeting structure and the student information around:

- The welcome introduction followed by overall impressions of the child and all they offer in your class community.
- Your overview of where the class is in terms of learning progressions and what's coming up as well as any expectations you have for notetaking and homework.
- Your view of the areas of strength and areas of growth for the child. Share data that is both visual and easily digestible for the time you have together.
- Your view on additional supports parents can offer at home to support the learning.
- Parent questions.

Remember that when you share, make the student data digestible. Keep the information clear and visual. If there's an IEP or 504, make it clear to the parents how those needs are serviced in the day-to-day. If they are an English as a Second Language student, explain their progress and areas of growth in terms of how the student receives support in the room or pullout services. Teachers love their takeaways from conferences and trainings, so have a takeaway of their student's information to provide them as well as the best ways to reach you.

> You are meeting a student's parents for the first time. How do you connect with them?

The Pulse Quickens

What if the parent or caregiver wants to continue beyond the scheduled meeting time? Be patient with them, but it is important to establish your boundaries. Let them know in an honest and supportive way that you must end the meeting, but they can email you or write their other questions down, and you will respond to them over the next 48 hours or schedule another time to finish the conversation virtually. How you close a meeting with a parent is just as important as how you open it.

What if the parent(s) is upset with me, either directly or indirectly? Oh, there will be times where they will be! There will be times that you are the target of their disappointment or downright displeasure. It is important to acknowledge their feelings and position, and remind yourself this is about the child at the end of the day!

Unless parents are in the field of education, they could not possibly be expected to know those inner workings and day-to-day aspects of a school environment. For them, when they have time with you and access to your thoughts and opinions, they are focused on having their questions answered and their problems or concerns solved. Sometimes that can happen in 15-20 minutes, but often it does not. When a parent has a concern, something has happened to their child, or their child has received consequences for something, or the parent has attempted to make contact with a member of the school staff without success. Some parents will continue to try and reach staff members about the issues at hand, some will go directly to administration, and some will go beyond that if they feel they have not been given a voice in the situation.

"We want help, not a fight. We shouldn't have to go above the school when we have questions about our children. The school is equipped to answer our questions, and there is no need for us to feel ignored just because we happen to be 'those parents' who are the ones emailing and asking questions about health and safety. We want to be partners, but we feel like what we have to say is irrelevant and that our needs are inconvenient for the school."
-Parent of Kindergartner and 3rd Grader

Okay, but Matthew, what do you do when things don't go as planned, and a parent feels like they haven't been heard, or responded to, or that their child is failing, or their social-emotional wellness is compromised because of another child in the class? In short, what if they are angry, and it is directed at you? What if a parent conference suddenly feels like a tug-of-war?

In my experience, this has happened, and more than likely you will also experience a parent, or parents, who come to a meeting with frustration in their hearts, a lot on their minds, and a willingness to let you know how they feel about it. I've seen this at every grade level, and the bottom line is that parents want to be seen for the role they have, respected for what they are upset about, and listened to in terms of the list they have brought to share. If the meeting is going sideways, and you are noticing a shift in their tone, language, volume, rate of speech, or body posture, apply the following strategies:

Navigating Blockages

- **Validate their emotional experience:** You can let them know you appreciate what they are sharing and that you understand they are feeling a certain way. Share that you are more than willing to work with them to determine a transparent course of action to be responsive to their, and/or their child's needs.

- **Listen to what they are trying to tell you, and restate it to them to confirm what you heard is what they meant:** For example, "What I hear you saying is that (child's name) feels like I'm not helping them on their social studies project, that I'm ignoring them, and they think I help others too much and don't help them enough. Is that right?" Again, behavior is communication, and while they will communicate verbally, paraverbally, and nonverbally, it will be up to you to not just hear them, but listen to what they need from you. Reviewing their feedback and/or requests with them will ensure everyone is aligned in the next steps.

- **Avoid the powerplay:** They may want you to know that they feel like you are not doing a good job, or there has to be a reason why their child doesn't like you, or they disagree with your lifestyle, or they are in charge, or they are a person with power, degrees, and money. I've heard them all, but it doesn't change the fact that time is short, and the child comes first. The redirection is bringing them back to how best to support the child. You may have a different opinion or disagree with something they have said, but it is never a good idea to attempt to argue back with a parent, question their parenting, or challenge their moral/ethical views. You need to be patient in the sense that you want to make them feel like by expressing their views that you have heard them and want to be responsive to supporting the child.

- **Choices and solutions:** When you've listened and reframed, be prepared to provide a few different choices for what can happen next to support the parent's concerns as well as explicit solutions. These can be written down and then email-shared with the parent post-meeting.

- **Pull the ripcord:** Everyone needs an escape plan, especially if something feels unsafe or that it isn't going in a positive direction. You need to be able to maintain your own boundaries, politely end a meeting, thank them for their time, and provide them your contact information to schedule another meeting. *"I very much appreciate you being here with me. You are wonderful advocates for your child, and I am sorry we aren't able to resolve everything at this time. I can hear that we still have a lot to work through which is fine, so while we are ending now, here is my contact information so we can schedule an upcoming time. That way I can invite additional support (administration, school counselor, reading specialist, team leader, content specialist, etc) so that the team and I are able to more fully address your concerns. I want to be able to do that for you and get this right for (child's name)."*

- **Follow up and find a way:** Make sure that the other members of your team supporting the student are copied on your messaging so everyone is connected with what is being shared, and always find a way to build that trust in your follow-up. Parents need to know that even though you have many students that this one, theirs, is a priority, and your response and the solutions you offer must reflect that.

Here is one, fictional sample of a message created post-conference for a concerned parent in a meeting that turned out to be emotionally charged with a lot of parent frustration. It could be adapted for various situations and translated for any family's language needs. It is framed in Heartleading language.

Opening greeting:

I wanted to first thank you for sharing (child's name) with me and for meeting this evening to discuss (child's name)'s progress.

While we addressed a lot of great things happening for (child's name) in the classroom, I know you also shared a lot of concerns about missing classwork, another student's behavior and its impact on (child's name), and some attention and anxiety concerns.

It was very important for me to hear you share those things, and it is equally important for me to let you know that student academic and social-emotional wellness are priorities for us here. Additionally, (child's name) deserves to be able to learn without disruptions, and I appreciate your patience as we make some adjustments to resolve that as well. I am sorry these issues exist, but I am happy to be partnering with your family, and our team here, to create solutions.

I am copying our school counselor and (child's name)'s teachers on this so that they too are connected with the work we will do to build supportive measures for (their) schedule. We are also going to offer some extra check-in time with counseling to put strategies in place to cope with these big feelings. A 13-year-old has a lot going on during middle school, and it is important they have a voice in their own care and people and places to share those questions and feelings with during the school day. I will contact you on Thursday with updates on each of your questions as well as what we have put in place around the other concerns you shared with me.

In the meantime, should you need anything, please contact me at the information below.

Gratefully,

Your name/title– (Include your information how your school requires it. Include school phone number/email.)

During those conferences, impromptu meetings, and the random quick conversations between parents and educators, so much can be shared without a single word being exchanged. These are moments where things can be made explicitly clear or become very confusing between parties. This can be especially true around people communicating from different cultures. An educator practicing cultural competence and an overall sensitivity for navigating the nuances of respecting people's different approaches to engaging with others brings the work of Albert Mehrabian (1972) to the forefront. A pioneer of non-verbal communication (NVC), Mehrabian's comprehensive research around people, interactions, and NVC would bring forth his "7-38-55 rule." Mehrabian stated that 7% of the meaning of feelings and attitudes happens through our words, the spoken communication; 38% is shared through tone and the voice; 55% of communication is provided through the body language we use, specifically our facial expressions. The research offered that human interactions primarily use face and voice to determine what emotions are being communicated in any given interaction.

Reading Between the Lines–Building Cultural Competency

- **Do your research:** Can you learn a greeting or other signs of respect in their language? Is there handshaking, hugging, both, or none? What is allowed or appropriate? How do the greetings (entrances) and goodbyes (exits) in words and behaviors play out between different groups? Are there resources in your school or system you can reach out to for support and guidance in preparing for a meeting? Do you need a translator with you? Have you made sure to schedule at a time where your meeting isn't affecting a significant cultural or religious event?

- **Body language:** (facial expression, eyes, proximity, body contact) Be aware of yours, and what messages you may be non-verbally sending. Did you cross your arms when they started speaking? Are you seated in a manner that has you placed physically higher than them? Is your body positioned where they are talking to/and only seeing your profile? Are you playing with your hands or tapping your feet and knees up and down? Where are your eyes, and are they hard or soft focused?

- **Paraverbal communication:** It's all about *how* something can be said, not the words that are actually used. This is impacted by tone, inflection, volume, rate of speech, and placement of emphasis on certain sounds.

- **Be clear and direct with what you say:** Incorporate the use of a translator if needed, and focus your statements around growth with a flexible mindset (e.g. "Ayla has learned 7 of her 25 sight words, and that's amazing. She hasn't gotten them all *yet*, but she is working hard on the next five right now. She feels so proud of her efforts!" "Lucas has not gotten this Spanish assignment into me yet, so I am providing him with a make-up session tomorrow during lunch and one after-school session. We can give him the time to make it happen. Here's a reminder note for his planner from me, and with your support tonight at home, I know we can help him get to me tomorrow and earn a grade that will bring up his overall average!")

A Heartleader seeks to partner and will create an appropriate response working to meet families where they are. "Adopting a partnership philosophy means sharing power and setting up mechanisms such as councils, committees, and focus groups. Giving families a voice in decisions and real jobs to do are convincing signals that the school recognizes and values parents" (Henderson et. al., 2007, p.56).

This is the *yes* that a Heartleader carries in their hearts–free of pride, humble and open. Yes, I am here to listen. Yes, we share the work and accountability. Yes, we have ways to respond to your needs. Yes, we support you unconditionally. Yes, together, we will create solutions that are fair and transparent. There will never be a simple solution for navigating parent perspectives for they are as unique and complex as the students served, but building the foundation together links you together in the service of their child.

Consider how you would respond to these challenging parent questions taken from a collection of teacher and administrator experiences:

- *"If he's failing, and missing 6 assignments, I didn't even know. Why didn't the teacher ever call me?"*

- *"How does she tell my daughter in front of her whole class that she is flirting with a boy on the screen? Why would she say that? She is nine years old, do you know how that makes me feel as a parent and teacher?"*

- *"He needs a desk, somewhere to just be his, and he can't sit on the couch all day. We don't have money to buy a desk or a little table, and he needs summer shirts and shorts. I'm not too proud to ask, can you do anything for us?"*

- *"Why does she even have a flash pass to see the counselor, and use the bathroom if the teacher tells her she didn't need to go or has to wait? We talked about all this in the meeting, right? So why couldn't she use her flash pass? She wet herself; she has a diagnosed condition, and I want to know why someone thinks that's okay to let happen."*

Doing the Best They Can

Parents show engagement with school in a variety of ways. Remember we talked about origins and stories? Many families, while deeply invested in school and education, aren't always able to get to a school during the day, make contact, or attend events. This does not mean they do not care or do not make their child's learning and success a priority. Frequently, work responsibilities, access to technology, childcare schedules, or their own personal experiences with schools may be reasons they are unable to engage in the traditional ways. By creating opportunities for parents and caregivers to share where, when, and how they receive information in order to be connected with schools you give them ownership in the community-building process and thus a stake in the creation of a relationship with you.

You can provide additional forms of outreach in order to make sure families get information and stay plugged into everything throughout the school year and summer. This generates a foothold in trust and an understanding between school leadership and parents/caregivers that says, *"We want you to be a consistent part of this in any way you can, thank you. When you need us we are here to support you and your child."*

A recent conversation I had with a parent started like this: *"Mr. Bowerman, you told me in our meeting you would call me today with an update, and you did. You kept your word and that goes far with me. Most people can't even do that anymore."*

You are bridge building your way to clearer and more transparent calls with families when you keep your word. In speaking with parents for over twenty-six years in K-12, here are a few of the things parents have directly shared with me about school, connection, and relationships. Imagine if that conversation went the opposite way.

"Mr. Bowerman, you told me in our meeting you would call me with an update, but that was last week, and I'm still waiting days later to hear from you. Why would you give me a promise but not keep it? Is that the approach of administration here? You couldn't take a few minutes just to let me know? My son's still afraid. He still doesn't want to come to school, and frankly, I want to know what you're going to do about it. How do I know you'll even do anything if you can't even keep your word to call me when you said you would?"

Either of those calls paints a very clear picture of the dynamics of relationships, priorities, and the type of trust a parent would feel towards their school leadership. Again, children remember and so do their parents. When you give your word, make sure you can keep it. Create agreements, but set boundaries with your parents and caregivers. It is important they understand they can have access to you, but there is a clearly defined process in place to make it happen. Make the aforementioned conversation the type they remember for all the right reasons, even when there are challenging topics.

Speaking of challenging, I have never met a school employee, myself included, who did not think that this work provides challenges in every shape and size. In K-12 education. from city to county, rural to urban, public to private, and everything in between, I have discovered a lifetime of beautiful and profound things that have happened, but every single day in the lives of students, staff, and families there are challenges that will emerge; there is no way to get away from that fact. We must strive to be preventative and work in responsive ways, but things happen, and when they do we are on the other side of a challenge, and we then react.

These challenges, pulled from parts of stories I have experienced or had shared with me over the past twenty six years will test you in many ways. They will force you to possibly question yourself, your morals, your feelings, or your own origin story.

The First Steps: Elementary Parents

"We were new, and our daughter was already having some trouble with her letters and what they sounded like. We like her teacher, but we already feel like she is falling behind, and she's a little scared to come to school."

"When I call, I want to know that someone on the other end cares and that they know my kid and can help me. We've been here two years, and they still don't know us."

"Yes, he's ten and has long hair, but they keep calling him a girl.

He's not a girl, and long hair is sacred to our culture. It's not right, and then the other two children putting yogurt on his back. What's going to be done to protect him, and let others know you cannot disrespect someone's culture like this?"

"I alone touch my child. No one else can touch my child, do you understand what I am saying? I did not give them permission and neither did he. Can you tell me why someone put their hands on my son today?"

This is elementary education, the foundational building blocks of a student's academic and social-emotional lives, right? So there is an elevated sense of urgency and concern for families with children so young and vulnerable. A formative time requires a formative approach to working through concerns when they are brought forward.

> Imagine the child is yours. The situation is one you are living or have lived. Regardless of your position, what would you need to hear? What would you need to see done next to restore your faith?

Navigating the Gray: The Middle Years Parents

"It's the cellphones, the constant texting, the apps, and the fact that they can go anywhere, see anything. It's hard to control, harder to stop. When we were kids someone spread a rumor, and some people heard about it. Now it goes live, or it gets posted, and the world knows everything about your kid, and they feel like life ends right then and there."

"People know middle school is way harder than elementary. They treat kids differently, kids treat one another differently, and it is a big shock. It was to us, and we don't know what we don't know. I don't know what to do, and she's been cutting herself alot, but she doesn't know I know about it."

"I sent the nude pictures, but they weren't of me. They were of my friend."

"I wanted to be kept in the loop about the situation on the bus, and we got a call, but I don't feel like enough was done and we're just not sure we can trust she's going to be safe. Who else can we speak with who can tell us she'll be safe?"

"You don't want your child going to a school where you, yourself, don't feel welcome. That doesn't feel good at all."

"I'm afraid to go home. I'm afraid all the time."

Middle school is rough, no matter the family. No matter the student. From the dangers of social media and puberty, trying to fit in, and a whole new set of emotional dynamics that can put any eleven to thirteen year-old, or any parent for that matter, into a tailspin.

> Consider how these middle school issues might have affected these students and parents. In your role, what's the next move? How do you respond in ways that validate their experiences and provide support?

The Path Towards Adulthood: High School Parents

"We appreciate you being supportive, but we're still trying to mourn our son. Do you understand that? We have to have a daughter now, when we've spent fifteen years with a son. A name change is one thing, but no one tells you how to just stop, and I'm not sure we know exactly what we do now. My husband can't even talk about it."

"Our best friend was killed last week at that block party shooting."

"It's messed up; I'm failing math, and I need this to graduate, but he won't let me do any make up work to bring my grade up."

"We felt like our family was more than just another number on a sheet last year. They took the time to know our kids, and our family, but now it's a new year, and this class isn't working for us. This teacher told my daughter she may be better off doing something in manual labor. That was his response when she told him she wanted to study law next year."

"My mom gave me the knife for protection. I'm not going to get jumped and not be able to defend myself. My mom said you can't defend me. No one helped me last time those girls caught me at the mall, now they're following me home."

"You're telling me he's failing, and I'm telling you he can't read, and no one's helping us, and this boy's almost seventeen, and he can hardly read. Didn't anyone wonder how he got this far? We've been asking for help for a long time, and now we're here, and you wonder why he broke that computer."

The world children are growing up in today is filled with opportunities and hardships many of us never dreamed of when we were kids. It almost makes the typical high schooler, on average, seem three to four years older than they are based on everything they are exposed to. There is a lot out there waiting for them, but it is this high school time when we have a chance to collaborate with our young adults who have a lot of different skills to offer; it is school that provides that final training ground to set them up for post-graduation success in a very fast-paced, constantly shifting world.

Let's get right to it. High school is the doorway, the gateway to a new set of directions that give students what they need to shape their future selves. It may be military or college, fire, police, the trades, or any other number of careers. Along these four years students lives are filled with situations that consistently work to pull them from their paths and dreams. Not every path is for everyone, and in this day and age, higher education is not the only solution for building a highly successful life. By the end of high school, these students are almost out of your reach in terms of school, almost done, but what you've read above is part of their reality, their experience.

> Consider your intervention—is it needed, and if so, how can you help rewrite the narrative in favor of hope, support, and that future success they deserve?

To me, these K-12 years represent such an opportunity for educators, and yet there is so much weight that goes with it. I feel like in my various roles over the years that it did not matter what title I had, or what degrees I had earned. The responsibility I carried for them was far more important and thus far heavier than anything else. It is this very point and the stories above that lead us back to the community building and the need for consistent, transparent communication from the very beginning of their schooling. It is critical that schools cultivate an approach whereby school to family communication is prioritized, and leadership learns the ways in which its stakeholders want to be communicated with. Furthermore, in communicating, it is always an exchange, and that feedback is vital to shaping true school improvement.

This sample tool for a parent survey was created to convey a message of partnership and transparency with the community; consider the following items in developing yours.

- Create in multiple languages to fit your community needs.
- Provide the survey during the first or second week of school at Open House.
- Let families know about the survey and where to find it prior to the event.
- Keep it specific but simple; 3-6 questions.
- Provide multiple formats to complete the survey.
- Create monthly, town hall meetings with your parent organizations to follow up on the data with dates/times posted, including a virtual option to attend.

Always know that families want to provide this information, but they may need multiple ways to communicate it. Some of the participants may want to be anonymous, which is completely okay. This type of open house survey can be set up in a Google form, as well as a paper version, or completed on a phone through your own QR code.

Open House Parent and Caregiver Survey

- What way do you prefer to receive information from the school? (Email, phone call, school text, newsletter, website, other)

- When you call the school, how are you treated?

- When you come to the school, how do you feel walking inside?

- When speaking to administration, teachers, or other staff, do you feel that your needs are heard and responded to?

- Does this school community act with the best interests of all races, languages, and cultures in mind? Why/why not?

- What can we do better?

Keep in mind the expectation would be that in collecting this vital data, it requires a school to face various potential realities about parent perception. It demands a response, tangible and visible proof, that a school takes parent voice seriously. It is critical to note that if you collect voice data from parents, you have a means by which to analyze, respond, and use it. After you and your school have come together to review and process the feedback, then actionable strategies can be created to address the voice data. These courageous conversations may require retooling of current mission or vision work, and/or adjusting practices currently in place. That's okay. Authentic work requires authentically facing perceptions about a school from the points of view of all its stakeholders.

From this initial voice data, the school should build teams to train those responsible for implementing the revisions with staff throughout the year. In this ongoing approach, leadership would communicate in a variety of ways, such as through your local parent-school organization, school website, letter from the principal, school newsletter, video chat, virtual office hours, etc., what the feedback was, and how the school would address it to support the broader community. This work would be revisited based on a timeline of response to the community.

For Heartleaders, community response is the most unifying type of response, whereby everyone is *in the know* in one form or another. How these connections are established, monitored, and maintained in terms of the business of school is different for every school and district, but it yields unlimited emotional capital in terms of school climate, culture, and student success. "You can try to speed the trust-building process, but feeling connected grows slowly and requires time for people to get to know each other. It happens in those small day-to-day-interactions… trust begins with listening" (Hammond, 2015, p. 77). School improvement is only genuine if everyone involved is connected in some measure to the work that will build and implement those improvement priorities and goals.

HEARTBEATS

Heartleaders prioritize parents and caregivers by:

- Elevating their voices and ideas in conversations.
- Recognizing that parents/caregivers show involvement and engagement in many ways.
- Understanding that all parents/caregivers want their children to be safe, successful, and happy in school.
- Encouraging parents/caregivers to bring their own origin stories to every aspect of school.
- Emphasizing that parents/caregivers bring tremendous insights, skills, and resources to the school experience; tap into those opportunities!

6. Supporting School Staff

"Heartleading is intentionally creating space for joy, connection, and community in schools. Leaders attending to school staff and their social-emotional needs–creating space for personnel to communicate about their own trauma and/or challenges, creating action plans to support teachers who may be struggling, and removing the stigma around mental health by being transparent and open about issues as they arise."

-Dr. Tracy Edwards

Literacy Strategist, Teach Plus Nevada Plus Fellow, Author

Being in education, through all of my roles, has been one of the greatest gifts I could have ever given myself and my family. If you are here on this journey with me and work with students in any capacity, you are an educator. The role defies anything you could learn in a college textbook or graduate school slidedeck. I don't even think the job description in applying to any school system can begin to prepare people for what they will encounter when they step into the K-12 universe. It is a profession as daunting as it is miraculous. Anyone who is, or who has ever worked in this capacity, regardless of the grade level, knows what we experience daily, and I love it. I just simply love the chance to be able to collaboratively engage in the work of building better learners and by extension, better people. It feeds my heart and helps to provide healing to those wounds in me, being able to give back and be a part of something so much greater than myself.

In all of my years as a student, there have been hundreds of teachers I have experienced, but I can count on one hand those who made choices to look out for me, to see me and learn about me, to challenge and change my life for the better. There were so many more who struggled with their own personal needs, incapable of de-escalating me, or working through my inability to understand numbers in a typical way. There were others who started the first steps with me but had difficulty deciphering who or what I was, and so they kept a kind but wary distance. I like to think many tried across the years, but as you probably are also thinking, there are those few, those special few in each of your lives, that overshadow the rest. They lifted you onto their shoulders to show you how you could rise towards some greater sense of yourself. Ultimately, from those heights you chose to serve and to educate. By working to educate, you made a silent vow to serve all children, to advocate and fight for their rights, and to safeguard their learning and their lives. It is a phenomenal thing you do every day.

Here you are now with me, exploring critical questions and practices, to shape and/or reshape your why as well as the work you do because of what you believe in. It's good you are here, and in supporting our educators, it is imperative to stress that none of us are alone in any of this. While often it is just you or you and your co-teacher or paraeducator standing up in front of 20 or 30+, there are networks of support throughout our profession to enrich you, protect you, and hear you out and send some love when you need it.

What I also need to say is that we are doing some incredible work nationally in building supports for students and developing additional ways to connect school and family. However, we have not prioritized those in our schools as much as we can around their care, and thus, in turn, their sustainability in this profession. When I consider the work of educators I have spoken with nationwide, these are some of the questions we have examined that need answers when supporting all school staff long term.

- In what ways are you addressing the social-emotional needs of you and your staff? What do you do when they are in need?
- What does your staff think, feel, and state regarding the school community?
- How is the staff voice represented in your school?
- How are staff trained to ensure academic, social-emotional, and anti-racism initiatives are implemented with authenticity and fidelity?
- What type of feedback is provided to build staff capacity in order to support both instruction and social-emotional teaching?
- What visible ways are staff supported and shown they are valued in your school community?

Heartleading prioritizes people, that human factor, in all interactions. The work of education is founded in service and connections; this is where we want to begin when talking about supporting school staff. We want our people taken care of, to feel safe, be able to have agency in their work, and to feel connected to the community in which they work.

Connection, as a strategy, comes in many forms, and the way you find out about how staff want to feel connected is to ask them, seek their guidance, expertise, and institutional knowledge, and use their feedback in the moves you make.

This is personal work: navigating people, building up staff, and establishing a community. The work of Heartleaders, from novices to well-trained veterans, places each person in positions where they may be operating trauma adjacent. Moving in such emotional conditions can also create considerable compassion fatigue, also known as vicarious trauma.

> Teachers' compassion fatigue is based on the premise that they actively give empathy to the real, implicit, or imaginary relief targets (students). In the process of providing material or emotional assistance to the relief targets (students), they suffer secondary trauma, which reduces their ability and interest in empathizing with the relief targets (students), the academic work burnout feeling emerges, and even changes in their original values and worldview occur, along with a series of physical and mental discomfort symptoms (Asquith, 2023, para. 6).

Educators, who now wear more hats than ever before, need to be supported as more and more of this comes to light. Cipriano and Brackett (2020) interviewed many educators about what they are facing, what they need, and the overwhelming conclusions focused on

"Connection is the energy that exists between people when they feel seen, heard, and valued; where they can give and receive without judgment; and when they derive sustenance and strength from the relationship."
-Brené Brown

>...the causes of stress and burnout are related to a lack of strong leadership and a negative climate, as well as increased job demands, especially around testing, addressing challenging student behaviors, a lack of autonomy and decision-making power, and limited, to no training, in social and emotional learning (SEL) to support educators' and students' emotional needs (Paragraph 10).

School staff must feel connected to the place and people (adults in this case) to truly feel empowered, and able to perform at a consistently high level. They must know their sense of physical and emotional self is being safeguarded.

This level of connection takes time: bridge-building with people, learning about them, and seeking to create understanding and some sense of common ground or purpose. Part of this building involves a clearly established mission and vision for a school. In addition, it demands transparent sharing of core values from school leaders in a space that prioritizes staff feedback and equity, as well as open dialogue about school goals and priorities.

These elements, combined with perception data and evidence-based research, frame an approach for the direction a school will move. Partnering with staff and parents can begin a process to place everyone on the same level playing field in terms of opportunity, communication, and accountability. None of this surprises school staff; they just want to know that administrations and school systems prioritize their health, safety, and professional growth as much as any other part of the system. Heartleading in schools as it applies to connecting with and supporting staff recognizes that:

- Every staff member brings their origin to the workplace and needs room to evolve.

- Staff deserve to have access to the tools and resources needed to effectively support a school building's operations and/or provide quality first instruction as well as the time to unpack those materials and supplemental professional learning as needed such as preparing to launch a new curriculum.

- Staff should be able to enter a culturally responsive safe space where they feel safeguarded, valued, and heard.

- Staff deserve time to establish peer connections in the workplace, as well as mechanisms to report needs.

- Staff should be celebrated through the various love languages with regard to their efforts, job performance feedback, and overall data-driven success with teaching and supporting students and one another.

School systems worldwide have sought to provide considerable efforts in social-emotional support for students, especially during the elevated conditions of the Covid pandemic over the past three years, but an ongoing question remains. Globally, what are we doing about the physical and mental health of school staff–our bus drivers, school counselors, building service workers, teachers, paraeducators, administrators, cafeteria staff, and our instructional specialists to name a few.

How are we creating and supporting psychologically safe spaces for school staff? This is a key question, but it has to start with you.

> A high-quality school climate can cause a teacher's sense of obligation to repay the organization...when teachers perceive that the school values his/her contributions and provides timely and appropriate support, then they will feel more obligated to repay the school (Shakeel et. al, 2021, p. 20).

I've struggled at times with centering myself amidst my daily responsibilities and developing some type of personal practice for my physical and mental wellness. Things become piled up, we become emotionally cluttered, our physical spaces mirror our internal ones, and the habits we have suffered as a result. Overwhelmed suddenly feels like a state of mind we've been renting space in for far too long!

To that point, I've been following some simple, but critical advice given by author and therapist Phyllis Fagel: "Calm the body to calm the mind" (Fagell, personal communication, September 2021). That is where I start a daily centering routine to calm myself amidst a profession that often comes at me at high speeds. Here are five ways I do it; maybe they can work for you as you develop your practice.

I continue to place myself in the uncomfortable position of challenging what I had not been doing to take better care of myself. I am working on leaning into the discomfort of my body when triggered to use my own tools to give myself grace to accept my limits and patience to love myself enough to work through the issues. "We often focus our energy, love, and care on the students. However, we don't often offer the same energy, love, and care to ourselves and to school staff members" (Carrie Viera, personal communication, March, 2021). Heartleaders extend this same approach to the people they interact with, and the personal inventory

Figure 3
Beginning the Day

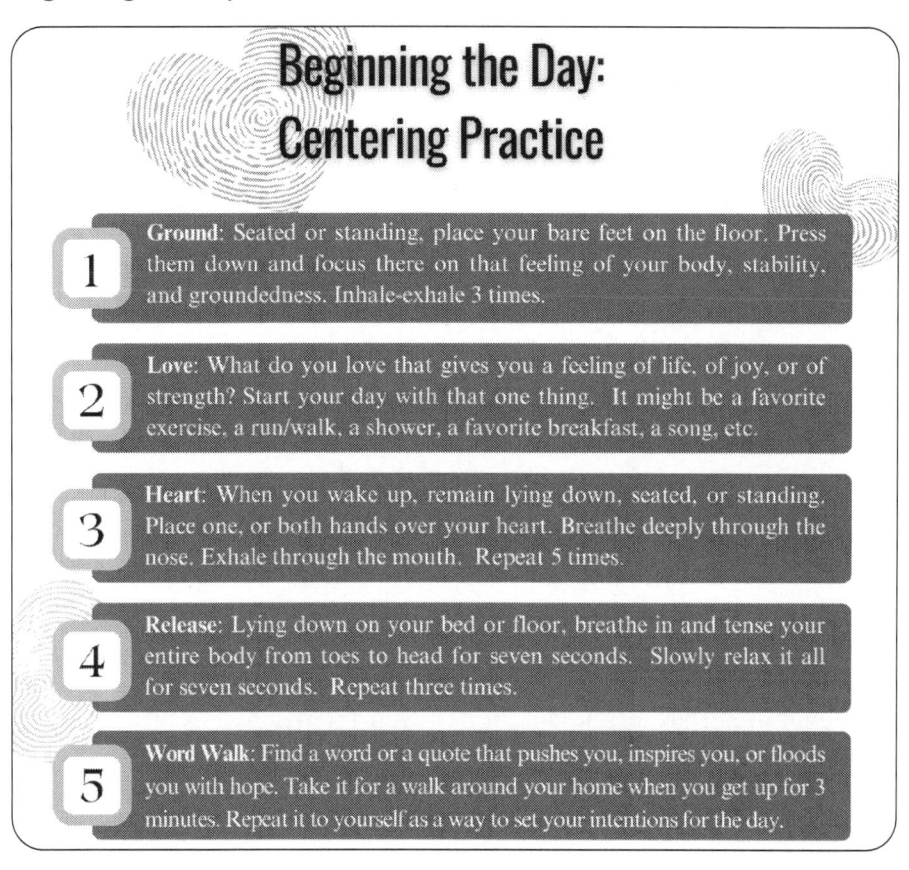

> ## Beginning the Day: Centering Practice
>
> **1** **Ground**: Seated or standing, place your bare feet on the floor. Press them down and focus there on that feeling of your body, stability, and groundedness. Inhale-exhale 3 times.
>
> **2** **Love**: What do you love that gives you a feeling of life, of joy, or of strength? Start your day with that one thing. It might be a favorite exercise, a run/walk, a shower, a favorite breakfast, a song, etc.
>
> **3** **Heart**: When you wake up, remain lying down, seated, or standing. Place one, or both hands over your heart. Breathe deeply through the nose. Exhale through the mouth. Repeat 5 times.
>
> **4** **Release**: Lying down on your bed or floor, breathe in and tense your entire body from toes to head for seven seconds. Slowly relax it all for seven seconds. Repeat three times.
>
> **5** **Word Walk**: Find a word or a quote that pushes you, inspires you, or floods you with hope. Take it for a walk around your home when you get up for 3 minutes. Repeat it to yourself as a way to set your intentions for the day.

process led me to meet new people and try some new things. Apart from my own extensive mental health practices, I have had the opportunity to explore mindfulness and meditation with support from Jeffrey Donald and Carrie Viera. Both are former educators who became certified yoga and mindfulness leaders; Jeff has gone on to lead mindfulness-based education and practices with Montgomery County Public Schools (MCPS) in Maryland, and Carrie has taken her mindfulness work into Restorative Justice where she leads MCPS and trains staff systemwide.

Creating practices grounded in taking care of ourselves really is essential to feeling healthy, remaining optimistic, and performing at optimal levels in our personal and professional lives.

> If staff members are stressed, students will experience, at worst the brunt of it, or at best, the side effects of it. Simply put, students have a greater chance of thriving when the adults who have the most direct influence on their lives are also thriving (Jeff Donald, personal communication, March 2021).

This work is not limited to an administrator or school culture, climate, or social committees; the question falls to all of us. How do you build trusting, safe, healthy, relationships in the day-to-day business of school? The following graphic shares some strategies you can use to support your role and responsibilities.

School staff are often caught between the desire to serve, to 'give their all,' and trying to hold it together, feeling like they are frayed and racing to keep up with falling behind daily and struggling to have anything left for themselves. Historically, teaching provided a fairly stable view of job security in terms of career and benefits, the job itself in the current climate feels neither certain nor very secure to educators.

Noted psychiatrist, Dr. Suniya Luthar shared that a lot of stress comes out of school staff consistently facing unpredictable circumstances. Unpredictability in life makes people anxious, and prolonged stress and uncertainty can lead to feelings of vulnerability or fragility in just about anyone. So there is great value to anything that contributes to people's sense of feeling safe and secure in their everyday

Figure 4
Taking Care of Staff and Yourself

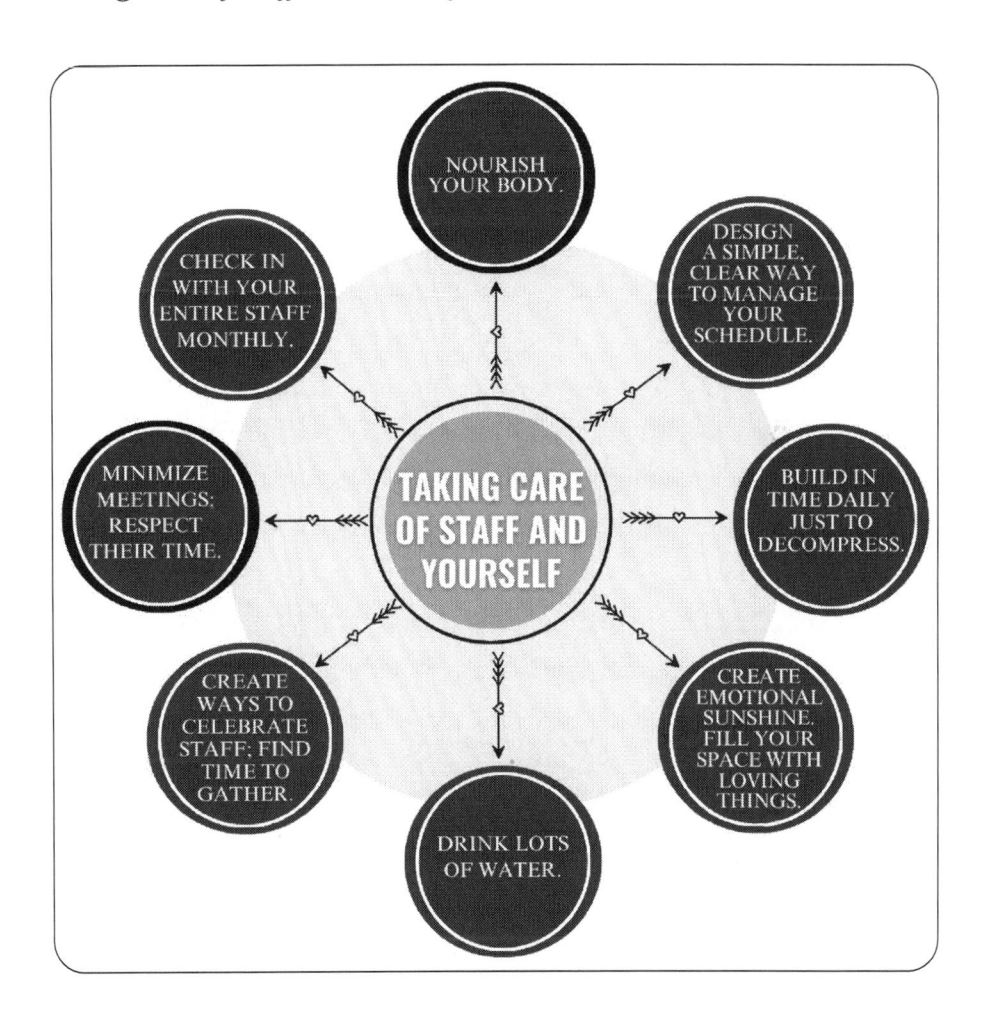

- NOURISH YOUR BODY.
- DESIGN A SIMPLE, CLEAR WAY TO MANAGE YOUR SCHEDULE.
- BUILD IN TIME DAILY JUST TO DECOMPRESS.
- CREATE EMOTIONAL SUNSHINE. FILL YOUR SPACE WITH LOVING THINGS.
- DRINK LOTS OF WATER.
- CREATE WAYS TO CELEBRATE STAFF; FIND TIME TO GATHER.
- MINIMIZE MEETINGS; RESPECT THEIR TIME.
- CHECK IN WITH YOUR ENTIRE STAFF MONTHLY.

TAKING CARE OF STAFF AND YOURSELF

work and home environments (Suniya Luther, personal communication, April, 2021).

We are really talking about designing ways to support psychological safety in a workplace. This idea that people, students, and staff alike feel like they are in a safe space and that they are also free to work, to learn, and to share without fear of reprisal, threat or punishment is imperative. I immediately began thinking about various staff and students I have collaborated with who, at one point, for a variety of reasons, shared that they felt unsafe or did not feel a sense of psychological safety in the school. Those were schools I had worked in and perhaps even contributed to those feelings at one point or another. What if my triggers elevated others? What if my own mental health work, during times when I was navigating unresolved grief and trauma, created issues for others? What if I was a source of anxiety for someone else? What if when someone needed me to elevate their social-emotional needs, I was not as responsive as I could have been? These questions pushed me deeper into reflections on myself and my practices, and the need to better understand psychological safety as a staff and student priority.

Exploring trauma, mental health, and the critical need for psychological safety as a human right brought to mind Zaretta Hammond (2015) and Daniel Goleman's work (1995) on culturally responsive training and the "amygdala hijack." The amygdala is the 'brain's guard dog' and the center of the fear system in the brain involved in emotional processing (Hammond, 2015, pp. 39-41); it reacts to any social or physical threat in less than a second. It has the authority in these moments to bypass the brain's communication system and send out signals in the form of cortisol–the bypass is the amygdala hijack. When this occurs all other cognitive functions such as learning, creative thinking, problem-solving, and rational thought all stop. The next part of the reactionary process is the fight, flight, freeze, or appease.

The daily life of an educator is complex, emotional, and weighted. Our schools are made up of adults from all over the world who have experienced some form of anxiety and/or loss or had an event trigger their own trauma. The work of the school, by its very nature, can be triggering. Many staff in schools are frequently caught in this hijack as a direct result of the trauma and/or social-emotional conditions they experience while also trying to balance the other aspects of their jobs and personal lives.

With the evolution of trauma-responsive teaching and leading and school-based social-emotional supports, the educational landscape has begun to shift in order to think preventatively and responsively act in order to support school staff with these needs. Courson (2021) provides several examples of national and international programs supporting the social and emotional needs of school staff. The Yale Center for Emotional Intelligence provides a RULER training tool for school staff focusing on guiding them through the understanding and implementation of an emotional regulation tool that places focus on recognition, understanding, labeling, expressing, and regulating emotion. Courson goes on to share that the application of this work provided data to support diminished teacher burnout and an increase in a positive outlook on their role as teachers using RULER (Yale Center for Emotional Intelligence, 2021).

An 8-week study of 58 Canadian and 55 United States teachers, called the Mindset Program (Roeser et al., 2013), was another emotional regulation project which focused on self-regulation techniques in the areas of self-compassion and mindfulness. The findings from the study supported the benefits for teachers in learning how to identify and manage the demands of their positions on a professional and personal level as well as develop strategies for building positive relationships with students (Courson, 2021).

Courson (2021) further shared that this support work is critical at the practical, hands-on level, to provide staff with the support, training, and implementation of intervention strategies for themselves in order to more effectively support students while safeguarding their own emotional lives. "More effort is needed to foster the emotional and social well-being of our teachers to improve teacher stress level to have positive effects on the quality of education" (Courson, 2013, p.12).

Here are Heartleading considerations in what it could look and feel like to have this level of support, and psychological safety, in the workplace.

Safe Spaces, Safe Faces

- Engage your leadership team around what a psychologically safe community would look and feel like, and then establish a plan to build one.
- Create a quiet, reflective space with your staff in the building designed just to focus on staff wellness.
- Provide a mechanism in the building for requesting employee assistance, and make it known that this is available to all staff and not connected with administration.
- Seek administrative support in stepping in to cover classes when a staff member needs a scheduled wellness break.
- Place the names, pictures, and contact information of school union representatives or elected faculty representatives in the staff mailroom.
- Create a list with staff of norms that are fluid but restated with in-

tention at every meeting so staff consistently hear what is prioritized when staff time is being used.

Staff want to hear and often need to see all of the following from administrators, team leaders, and even from one another. How could you use them? There are many ways to communicate; consider the manner in which each could be shared.

Figure 5

Match Your Say and Do

Match Your Say and Do

What You Say	What You Do
You matter.	Make this visible in the building. Create banners, wall art, etc. to make it well known, and provide a monthly message to each staff member about something great they did.
We believe in creating consensus around school-based decisions.	When you ask staff for opinions, make the information visible for all, and then use it to shape changes.
We implement and follow policies and procedures with fidelity because we respect you, your voice, and your position in this school; we use policy because it will protect you.	Create a working school handbook with your staff that is actually used, referenced, and consistently engaged with throughout the year.
We will respect your time and not waste it; we will meet when we need to.	If it can be sent in an email without scheduling a staff meeting, do that. If it can be a hybrid option and that works better for a specific occasion, try that for your staff.

What You Say	What You Do
When things get tough, and there will be times that they do, we will do everything we can to support and help you.	Provide staff with a way to request time to step out of their classroom for a break. Coverage will be provided.
We will provide feedback on the work you provide to build your capacities.	Schedule time with teams, and give them coverage, so they can visit colleague's classes and informally observe them to provide feedback.
As staff: how can I/we make your school experience better?	Design a way with staff input to collect that information, and then do it. Make sure they know that is an ongoing affirmation of their hard work.

Staff want more than just hearing it. They need to see all of those nice ideas lived out in actions. Here are some ways I prioritize this work in speaking my truth to action–Heartleaders should always keep these in mind.

Figure 6

Ideas Into Actions

Have a GREAT day on purpose!
Beliefs are lived through actions!

Make Your Love Visible
Model what you ask staff to do.
Be visible in hallways and classrooms.
Be on time; honor your obligations.
Keep your word and follow up.

Keep Your Heart Open
Share your mistakes; build solutions together.
Be curious about what staff has to offer.
Ask questions; listen authentically.

No Staff = No School
You are only as strong as your people.
They deserve to feel and be safe; create conditions with them to achieve this goal.

Pulsecheck Your People
Stop by rooms; check in with staff daily.
Build their capacities by seeing them work.
Keep feedback clear and actionable.
Create professional development based on what staff want and need.

Heartleaders are in a constant state of collaboratively building and rebuilding the foundations of an equitable, trusting, and safe, school community. In order for a school to run at optimal levels of academic and social-emotional success, there must be authentic buy-in from staff. A large portion of that buy-in has to do with them wanting to be in that school community, feeling good about where they work, why they work there, and how they are valued as an employee.

Educational research continues to draw direct correlations between these items and the need for staff to feel safe, be able to express their ideas, receive training and feedback that supports their role, and feel that their time and position are respected and used fairly and appropriately. In order to begin the initial steps for collecting staff voice, check out the QR code for your Preservice/Week One Staff Google Survey Tool.

HEARTBEATS

Heartleading makes sure that staff are respected, valued, and heard. Your school staff:

- Are vital and each plays a role in the community.
- Have stories too and with those stories come a lot of emotional investment and self-protection.
- Need to be safeguarded. As much as children's safety is made a pri-

ority in schools, staff are trained to protect them through various safety protocols, but we must make sure, as systems, that those protocols also prioritize the safety of staff–they deserve to go home too.
- Want to be treated fairly. From leave slips and coverage to evaluations, the processes in place should be equitably designed to support every staff member. When questions arise they should have access to the same contractual support as everyone else in their role.
- Strive to help students. No one is just jumping in for a paycheck and glory; as a whole, school staff want to do what's right for children.
- Must be plugged into the pulse of the school and part of communal decision-making processes. It becomes insulting to them when they are simply told what to do without being collaborated with on decisions that affect them.

7. The Emotional Aperture

"You are an aperture through which the universe is looking at and exploring itself."

-Alan Watts

Aperture

An *aperture* is "space for light to pass into and through" (Merriam-Webster, 2021). This word is often associated with a camera lens. There are different stops and sizes within cameras that allow light to transfer in different ways. Light allows us to *see*, and if we can take the light in and allow ourselves to be its conduit in our leadership, then the light surges by reflecting us and sharing it outward. The more of it we let in, the more we are able to find our own way and illuminate the way for others...the work of Heartleaders. I feel this approach to leadership asks us to not only use our literal sight but also how we see with our hearts–the emotional aperture.

The Emotional Aperture

The emotional aperture is the space in our hearts from which we can perceive and perceptually see the emotional qualities of people, places, and events around us. It requires being truly present in the moment and open to the feelings of others. Whereas the aperture is an actual structure that has a form and literal housing or shape, the heart's opening is perceptual, a concept from which we can focus our emotional energy on becoming open to the opportunity to experience and exchange emotional information and experiences with others.

As Heartleaders, in order to perceive and receive with our hearts, it asks us that we are:

- Emotionally available
- Compassionate
- Bringing authenticity to the experience
- Engaging empathetically

These four principles bring me back to love, and I am reminded of the Dalai Lama (2010) and his belief that compassion and love bring about the greatest happiness because our nature as human beings cherishes them above all things. The need for connection and love lies at the very heart of our existence. Love and compassion are necessities, not luxuries, and without them humanity cannot survive.

> The greatest degree of inner tranquility comes from the development of love and compassion. The more we care for the happiness of others, the greater our own sense of well-being

becomes. Cultivating a close, warm-hearted feeling for others automatically puts the mind at ease. This helps remove whatever fears or insecurities we may have and gives us the strength to cope with any obstacles we encounter. It is the ultimate source of success in life (Gyatso, 2023, para. 4).

This need to embrace compassion and love with our whole heart comes directly as the act of interdependence and our innate need for profound interdependence which we all share with one another. I have found in my healing and learning that engaging with others with these intentions in my words and actions, even when facing challenges, can be transformative.

> The Dali Lama's thoughts really hit home for me. Think of a profound quote or idea that you use to ignite your passion for this work and please place it here to come back to when you need it.

The Aperture, a Hobby, and a Love at First Click

I was first captivated by the concept of aperture, of an opening letting light pass through into the camera body, some fifteen years ago when I started collecting and experimenting with antique cameras and learning about their design. The shapes of the lens, when they were invented, and how they capture or collect images captivated me. In short, their origins. I collect stories like I collect antique cameras, and I have discovered that as stories have beginnings, middles, and endings, cameras and their lenses have their small, medium, and wide story-apertures.

To illustrate the connection, if the school is the camera, you can audit the picture and adjust the lens of the school's mission, vision, practices, and everything that goes into its community to determine which aperture the school was seeing itself and its impacts through. The observations of its aperture could be based on a variety of data sources like personal observations, the school's mission and vision, community walks and talks, auditing programs or policies, classroom observations and building tours, collecting voice data, as well as data collection around academics, behavior interventions, academic interventions, and additional programs at the school.

With the knowledge of what aperture was being used, conversations with stakeholders could take place around the aperture and what is needed to move the school towards its widest view by providing what would be needed to highlight the school's success as well as areas for growth. When I talk about aperture, I will continue to focus specifically on the types of openings connected with it: limited or small view, medium view, and wide or large view; the overarching view is guided by the emotional aperture and the information and experiences we collect around it.

Adjusting the Emotional Aperture

To further explain the principles that frame Heartleading and the emotional aperture, I discussed my work with four educational leaders embedded in teaching, leadership, mental health, educational advocacy, professional development, and reform. Each, from their respective educational platforms, provided insights into this work. Dr. Rachael George serves as the Executive Director of Elementary Programs in the Oregon Trail School District and is a former elementary and middle school principal as well as an adjunct professor, consultant, speaker, and author of *She Leads* and *Principaled*. Dr. George acknowledged the critical need for love-based leadership in schools and continued training for staff around social-emotional and trauma-responsive supports.

I shared my view of the emotional aperture and asked her to define emotional availability as she sees its applications in this work. She shared that an educator must be stable and balanced in their personal and professional lives. While she acknowledged how difficult this can be, she shared that it is only when that work is done that you are able to help others process their emotions or help when they are in crisis or 'flip their lid' without it impacting you. She further stated, "The key to being emotionally available for students, staff, and parents is that it is about having and maintaining boundaries with your life and relationships while also being able to care for others" (George, personal communication, January, 2021).

Desmond Mackall, Maryland School principal, leadership team member of Building Our Network of Diversity (BOND), and a doctoral student at Bowie State University shared his view on compassion in education citing the belief that an educator won't always know everything about someone. Most of the time you won't, and you don't need to, but you do need to listen. Desmond stated, "We listen to people–we hear their personal stories, their family stories, their student stories, so when we are present with them, we begin to understand them as people, and that's compassion to me" (Mackall, personal communication, January, 2021). He went on to say that people who want to show compassion to others need to be able to move beyond their own lens in order to really see a person and to make sure they feel seen and heard. "I don't have everyone else's lens, and so I have to be prayerful with families and with staff. I don't have their experiences, and so I pray for the wisdom to widen my aperture, so people feel valued, and they feel heard, whether or not we agree or disagree in the process" (Mackall, personal communication, May, 2022).

Thinking about his experiences as a student of color, a teacher, and now a principal, he would go on to offer that compassion asks you to reflect on your own core values and to remember everyone walking through that door may not share yours, but it is not about that. It is about being compassionate enough to be there to listen to them, to take a step back, pray for that wisdom and space, and to acknowledge what they come to you for. "You cannot do this job effectively without compassion. You can have passion and drive, but without compassion there is no relationship, there's no connectedness between you and stakeholders, and you have to have it to be in a school, and do this work" (Mackall, personal communication, June, 2020).

No stranger to classrooms or engaging in discussions around community, authenticity, and vulnerability, I was fortunate to connect with Alexis Shepard when we both presented at the Teach Better 2022 Conference. Alexis, who also goes by her brand name and the name of her podcast "The AfroEducator," is a South Carolina teacher, speaker, blogger, and wellness coach who was all in when introduced to my Heartleader training. Finding parallels in our work around love-based education, equity, kindness, and self-care, Alexis and I hit it off as we discussed her work in identifying strategies for reducing teacher burnout, reigniting joy in one's work, and being an advocate for teacher self-care.

As she was in my presentation, I wanted to get her insights into the nature of the emotional aperture and how authenticity plays into this work we both understand and love so much. Alexis shared that to be authentic in this work, you must first have clarity around your core values and be able to lead from those.

> When I was a classroom teacher, one of the most important things to me was to help my students become more compassionate and empathetic human beings. So every decision that I made, both instructional and non-instructional, was rooted in that core value. So living and loving authentically is about making decisions that are rooted in a clear purpose, and hopefully, that purpose is built on creating a more equitable, just, kind society (Shepard, personal communication, November, 2022).

On the topic of empathy and its connection to this work, I spoke with Dr. Byron McClure, founder of Lessons for Social-Emotional Learning

(SEL), National Certified School Counselor, author, keynote speaker, and 2019-2020 Whole Child Award winner. Dr. McClure stressed the need for authenticity in education and that empathy must be authentic to be exchanged. He feels that the acts of teaching and leading can only be successful if they are grounded in an empathetic approach to working with children and shares, "Empathy is authentically listening, understanding, and wanting to better understand others. My motto is that leaders must lead with empathy. To truly serve, it's one of the most important assets a leader might have" (McClure, personal communication, December, 2021).

To build one's heartleading capacities, it is important to identify which emotional aperture (narrow or small view, medium view, or wide or large view) is being implemented, and it begins with your own lens. Recognizing and engaging with your personal emotional aperture as a Heartleader is a healthy way to develop your mindset and approach to this work. Use the QR code for your Emotional Aperture Resource.

> Are you viewing your role, your work, and your relationships, through a small, medium, or wide emotional aperture? Which area of the emotional aperture is most developed in your practices? Where can you grow?

♡⁄ₗ HEARTBEATS

Heartleading is never performed in isolation. You want to expand your vision in all directions.

- It takes time, honesty, and effort in developing your aperture so that it remains wide open.
- Being compassionate begins with showing compassion towards yourself and your own wounds and healing.
- Becoming emotionally available is risky, and it takes work on yourself. The investment, although filled with a lot of self-reflection and vulnerability, is worth the personal payoff.
- You can always grow your aperture and along the way pulse check yourself, and clean the lens on your heartview.
- For this emotional aperture work to take root, it requires buy-in, transparency, and consistent messaging and communication.
- There is always light once you have looked for it. Here is a hint, it has always been with you. Once uncovered, the next quest is to learn how to give it to others.

"To support families' dreams, educators must demonstrate their belief that parents can help their children achieve them. First, we need to find out what those dreams are and figure out how to support families in realizing them."
~Beyond the Bake Sale, Anne T. Henderson, Karen L. Mapp, Vivian R. Johnson, Don Davies

8. Pulsecheck

Pulse racing, blood pressure rising, adrenaline pumping, nerves jumping, breathing quick and shallow. These are some descriptions of what the brain, heart, and overall body do when situations and circumstances become elevated or emotionally charged.

Stop, pause, breathe...PULSECHECK!

I asked author, speaker, and therapist Phyllis Fagel to provide her insights for you at this point. She is an expert on the pulsecheck and spends her time assessing and triaging in school by providing love, feedback, and guidance to students and staff. She also serves in private practice.

I work with a plethora of school counselors, and it's important to introduce your students to their counselors and their locations in the building when school first starts. This way students know the location of an emotional support person in the building as they transition and begin a new year.

In addition, plan with your school counselor(s) to have them visit your homeroom class the first week. Connections are critical in this area, and it is important to eliminate stigmas around visiting a school counselor. Students should know it is always okay to have thoughts and feelings, as well as a person and place to share them while at school.

I'd like to have Phyllis share her perspective with you now.

Phyllis & the Pulsecheck

When Matthew asked me to write a "Pulsecheck" section for his book -- and in the middle of a pandemic -- I felt paralyzed. I wondered, how could I possibly create the perfect bridge between chapters on Heartleading and Heartache? How could I match Matthew's trademark authenticity and ability to relay concrete strategies? And as a school counselor, what could I offer leaders in the midst of navigating one of the most intense and difficult experiences of their lives? And then I thought about what educators have been sharing with me since March of 2020. *"I feel so helpless... My students need me, but their needs are so great... I'm not trained as a mental health counselor... What if I do more harm than good?... Schools can't be everything to everyone... This is too much... I'm dealing with burnout and my own 'stuff,' so how am I supposed to support staff and students in crisis?"*

You're right. It is too much. You're in an impossible situation and can't be everything to everyone. The burnout is real. Most of you are not trained to deal with mental health issues, and adults and kids everywhere are struggling mightily. *And yet...*

About that "and yet." While everyone expects me -- a licensed counselor -- to be a first responder when students suffer trauma, the unspoken truth is that every adult in the school is a first responder right now. That's a lot of pressure.

You already have a ton of responsibilities, not to mention your own life stressors. (And that, by the way, was true long before you had to help kids living through a pandemic.) But I also know you're reading this book because you want to be a source of strength and love for children, and I'm here to say that that's a realistic, attainable goal. You don't need any special training to be someone's "person," and that's true regardless of your own emotional baggage. In fact, as Matthew's origin story illustrates, sometimes the bumpier your path, the greater your relational superpowers. Children are exquisitely attuned to authenticity, and they know when someone *gets it*.

Regardless of your past or present stressors, however, you can't tap into a well of empathy if it's dry, and let's be real, educators are pretty tapped out right now. So let's hit the pause button for a moment to take your emotional temperature. If you need help getting in touch with your internal life, the psychotherapist, Dr. Tina Payne Bryson, world-renowned speaker, author of No-Drama Discipline and co-author of *The Whole Brain Child*, recommends putting one hand on your belly and one hand on your heart, then asking yourself: "What do I need right now?" It's a form of self-nurturing that might help you realize, for example, that you're lonely and would benefit from calling a friend, or that you're feeling down about a negative exchange with a student and could use some reassurance from a trusted colleague.

Once you've taken stock of your emotional state and personal needs, you'll have an easier time lightening a student's emotional load. This may come more naturally to some of you than others, but the good news is that helping a child in crisis can be operationalized, meaning there are specific ways adults can respond when a child is in crisis. It's both an art and a science. There is the relational piece, which comes from trust, warmth, and care, and there are concrete, evidence-based ways to help children cope with distress, and get to the problem-solving stage. Some of my favorite tips are in the following graphic.

One of my favorite ways to bolster students' confidence is to ask them to come up with two strengths for every perceived weakness. A boy who feels bad about his learning challenge, for instance, might realize that his struggles have honed his empathy and work ethic. I've yet to meet any magical human -- adult or child -- who feels competent and secure all of the time, but that's not something kids understand intuitively. So be clear that there can be no peaks without valleys, and let them see you double down on your strengths instead of fixating on your weaknesses. Tell them when you seek help; they'll be far more likely to take you at your word when you say you want to help them. And while you're at it, do the same for your colleagues. You'll not only kick off a positive and nurturing cycle, but you'll also help your students. After all, children only tend to do as well as the adults in their orbit.

Phyllis Fagel, LCPC

Figure 7

Five Ways to Create a Safety Net for Emotionally Struggling Students

5 Ways to Create a Safety Net for Emotionally Struggling Students

1. **Self-identify as a helper.** At the beginning of the semester, explain to students you're not an expert in mental health but can be the bridge and help get the support they need. Define terms such as anxiety and depression, talk about what kinds of problems and symptoms require adult intervention, be clear that you want to help them, and if you refer them to a school counselor, walk them to that individual's office and help them relay their story.

2. **Share your own failures and talk about how you recovered.** Maybe you forgot to prepare a lesson, had to improvise, and spent an entire day feeling incompetent but went for a walk after work and kept reminding yourself that everyone makes mistakes.

3. **Help them label their feelings and then validate them.** That doesn't mean you necessarily agree with a child's assessment of a situation or approve of their behavior. It simply means you understand. You might say, "I would be angry too if I thought my teacher had purposely embarrassed me in front of everyone." When kids know what they are feeling and don't feel judged, they can get to the problem-solving stage.

4. **Normalize student insecurities whenever possible.** I have my students do the iceberg activity that prompts them to share what they think others see as opposed to what they actually feel beneath the surface. You can do this anonymously and then share answers with a larger group. It's a way to help students understand that no one's life is perfect, and everyone is plagued by self-doubt at some times. You can access this activity through any of the resources QR codes found throughout this book.

5. **Exhibit unconditional positive regard.** That means you really see your students and acknowledging them for everything they are. For example, a girl who has a tough time sustaining attention to detail also may have a knack for visualizing the big picture or bringing dynamism to a class discussion. A boy who loves to stir up drama might have a precocious sense of humor or tremendous self-awareness.

Feel free to jot down a few takeaways from Phyllis's Pulsecheck! Your heart and mind will thank you for it!

Pulsecheck Notes

❤️ HEARTBEATS

Heartleading as a practice keeps your finger on the pulse of your student, colleague, and community needs; it prioritizes their social-emotional lives and health. Phyllis reminds us:

- When working with students in any capacity, make sure they know how to access the school counselor, psychologist, and other mental health supports in your building.
- Work with those specialists to have them in spaces where they become everyday people to students–accessible, available, and engaged in various aspects of their school lives.
- You don't need any special training to be someone's person.
- Give yourself permission to feel; take your own emotional temperature. You'll need to fill yourself before you're able to be empathetic towards others.
- There are both relational and concrete strategies to support students in distress, and all of it can be learned without any special prior expertise.
- Use the 5 step safety net provided by Phyllis Fagell.
- No one feels competent and secure all the time, and that is okay. Double down on your strengths instead of fixating on your weaknesses.

9. Heartache

Creating Space and Balance in Times of Loss and Hope

"To serve school communities with love is to BE love to those you serve, no matter the circumstances…you smile at all, maintain a positive attitude along the way, because we don't know what that positivity can do for those we lead, for those we serve, those we teach. We only know that we love others because others might not be loving themselves and need that one ounce of hope to tell them, 'It's going to be okay.'"

-Laura Rizzo, School Counselor, Speaker & Developer

Heartache has been scientifically proven to cause significant stress, both physical and emotional. It was demonstrated that an experience of social exclusion activated neural regions typically associated with physical pain distress. Research has demonstrated that other types of socially painful experiences, such as experiences of social loss, can activate these pain-related neural regions as well. Our work in meetings, classrooms, offices, and communities shows us it is all connected--what we think and feel, how it affects us, and how it plays out in our everyday lives (Eisenberger, 2020).

We are social creatures designed to pair, group, or form attachments and make connections with other people. Our general nature is to seek out interaction with others as a species. Our emotions, while a chemical process, manifest physically as a result of the relationships we do or do not have with others in the world. These are universal truths experienced by human beings the world over. "Being socially connected is our brain's lifelong passion; it's been baked into our operating system for tens of millions of years" (Wolpert, 2013, para. 3).

When we cannot connect, we as a species experience a variety of reactions: loneliness, confusion, emotional and physical discomfort, or pain to name a few. "People describe sadness as heartache; the link between sadness and physical pain such as heartache has been empirically proven; however the mental foundations that support the connections between sadness and pain remain unclear" (Shirai & Toshi, 2019, para. 1).

Heartache, or heartbreak, has been used as a descriptor to paint the intense physical and emotional suffering, the actual pain, a person experiences as a response to some form of loss or disconnection. It has not been uncommon in my work with families to hear about high blood pressure, marital struggles, depression, massive panic attacks, job loss, pregnancy challenges, insomnia, and other physical and psychological needs. I am sure these same debilitating challenges are ones you have also heard in the stories of your communities.

The voices from my communities have shared many examples of heartache like love, hope, and loss over my career in education. Do any of these sound familiar to what you may have experienced in your communities?

"We are hurting. A lot has happened to us."

"This is her third accident this week."

"We all just sleep in the one room, on the floor."

"It's like a pain in my chest that won't go away."

"My heart hurts…"

"My grandma lived with us. She died from coronavirus; we shared a room."

"She just comes home from school and starts crying; we don't know what to say."

"We know things will get better, but we can't help but wonder when."

"He won't go to the bathroom or eat his lunch. He holds it all in."

"After I lost my job, we lost the apartment, and now we've been in the shelter."

"Can you guarantee that you can keep my child safe?"

The Cost

Those are real words, lives, and stories, and whether they come from something eight months or eight years ago, we know there is still hurt there, feelings of loss mingled with the never ending process of healing and recovery. Often there is anger there along with guilt, confusion, and the inability to let go. How

> "Trauma often shatters belief systems and robs people of their sense of meaning. In doing so, it forces people to put the pieces back together… rebuilding beautifully those parts of their lives and life stories that they could never have torn down voluntarily."
> — Jonathan Haidt, The Happiness Hypothesis

do we know this? Because we have been there ourselves, and through our own experiences, we too understand a hurting heart; we enter this profession, I believe, because we also work towards healing hearts. There is nothing in our experience, however, that can prepare us to think we know what someone else has been through or is going through, but it is an opening to forming a compassionate, empathetic bond for what they are bringing forward from their experience as it parallels with the potential similarities as yours.

Heartleaders bind their service to intentional behaviors with love as the guiding idea: love for self, love for others, love for taking on one's role in the community. However, using a word like love can sometimes make people feel uncomfortable or uncertain. This is understandable given the world's unique and complex relationship with the word and the diversity of both philosophy and action around it. So I approach the word as *sacred*, bringing respect, a healthy dose of caution, and my origin work to its use in school and community spaces. In acknowledging people's individualized and often complex relationships with the word, I work to explore its use gently with others, working from the edges in as we navigate conversations and relationship work in the day-to-day of our school experiences. To me, Heartleading and love are as closely aligned as connection and relationships; they are bound to one another in the field of education. It is through love that education is possible, and Perry & Szalavitz (2017) speak of loving others by identifying love for self stating that "the truth is you cannot love yourself unless you have been loved and are loved. The capacity to love cannot be built in isolation" (p. 262). While this is certain, as an educator interacting with children and adults, clear boundaries must be established, shared up front, and safeguarded.

The Ethics of Loving

Love as an action is often associated with intimacy in one form or another across cultures including kinship, romance, brotherhood and sisterhood through military service and/or combat. This includes expressions of physical and emotional affection that one would reserve for a partner, spouse, close friend, or family member. We are not looking to express love in this way or to connect with staff, students, or families on that type of love level. When Heartleaders speak of love, yes, it is certainly personal and absolutely emotional but still grounded in the professional expectations that guide staff behavior when working with children, families, and other staff. There are still guidelines and boundaries established; that cannot be emphasized enough.

Schools must be able to communicate guidelines around how teachers and students can interact, especially around contact. Leading researcher Alex Shevrin Venet (2021) asks vital questions around establishing boundaries: "Are teachers allowed to hug students? To share their home or cell phone numbers? To drive students in their cars?" (p. 153). We are not our students' parents, guardians, or caregivers and cannot claim to be; it would be naive, egotistical, and dangerous to think, even in the most extreme of cases, that we are saving students from themselves or others. That is not our role in providing love. This must always be clear in our words and behaviors.

"Relationships are the agents of change and the most powerful therapy is human love" (Perry & Szalavitz, 2017, p. 260). We may 'love' them like our own children, but again, they are not our actual children and still need to be approached as our students. For new and veteran school staff, the issues of boundaries and boundary-setting are critical when being onboarded as a first year teacher. It is important that you also speak with your school administrations, union representatives, etc. around expectations for some of these areas with students. The various grade levels (elementary vs. high school) provide differing nuances to all of these (e.g.--a student's parent is in a car accident, and the parent and your administration give you permission to drive the student home). Here are some considerations to maintain clear boundaries with students, and bring awareness to the interpersonal dynamics of adult-student interactions.

Healthy Boundaries–Protecting Yourself, Safeguarding the Student

Physical Boundaries	Do not have meetings alone with a student. Make sure another staff member is present, or your door is open with another staff member able to see you. Maintain an awareness of your proximity in relation to students and their bodies. Identifying males and females when addressed about sensitive subjects (e.g.--what they are wearing) should be done by a same-identifying sex staff member.

Emotional Boundaries	Do not publicly shame, tease, mock, or use sarcasm with students. Your job is to support, guide, and teach them, but you are not their peer in your role. Be aware that in connecting with students and healthy relationship building that you are a professional, and there must be limits to sharing common bonds vs. trying to create an emotional connection.
Behavioral Boundaries	Do not engage in social media with K-12 students; if there are academic-related interactions that happen via school email, make sure the parent is directly copied. You should not give out your personal information such as cell phone number to a student. You should not leave campus with students and go places with students or drive them places as a general practice.
Supportive Strategies	Create another high-level form of praise without touching (play their theme song, ring a bell, provide an incentive). Set up dedicated times with parents to conference about their child. Avoid talking about students in public, non-school settings, or engaging with other parents about students that are not theirs. If a student tells you something that requires a child protective services call, and you are not a school counselor, you need to immediately refer that child and have the counselor get them to provide support. Maintain a culture of respect and demonstrate your cultural competence in your awareness of various social norms, customs, and behaviors for interactions and boundaries.

School systems need to be able to build teachers by way of providing professional development on problems of practice and ongoing staff training to relational issues, especially in the first three years of teaching, around boundary-setting, and maintaining specific, healthy expectations for interactions in relationships. Rego & Fader (2021), in examining the role of love and communication in cultivating healthy relationships, share that a critical element of communication is learning about the ways in which people actually receive and process information. They talk about mindful listening and explain:

> focusing your attention entirely on them while not judging what they are saying, not getting lost in your own thoughts, not jumping to conclusions, and not listening to them just to respond to your own thoughts…it is especially relevant when it comes to receiving love, affection, or appreciation (p. 61-63).

Your Love Language

As it is a nuanced topic, and different the world over, consider some of these questions in your practices around love and the languages.

- Are you able to offer your love from a culturally competent place of giving? In what ways can you broaden the lens, and increase your capacities in this area?
- What is the love language you use to show others you care for them? Is it different with different people?
- Which love language makes you feel appreciated? Again, is it differ-

ent with different people?
- Which love languages are you uncomfortable using? Why? Are there any cognitive distortions present?
- Which love languages do you feel uncomfortable exploring? Why?

Figure 8

Five Love Languages

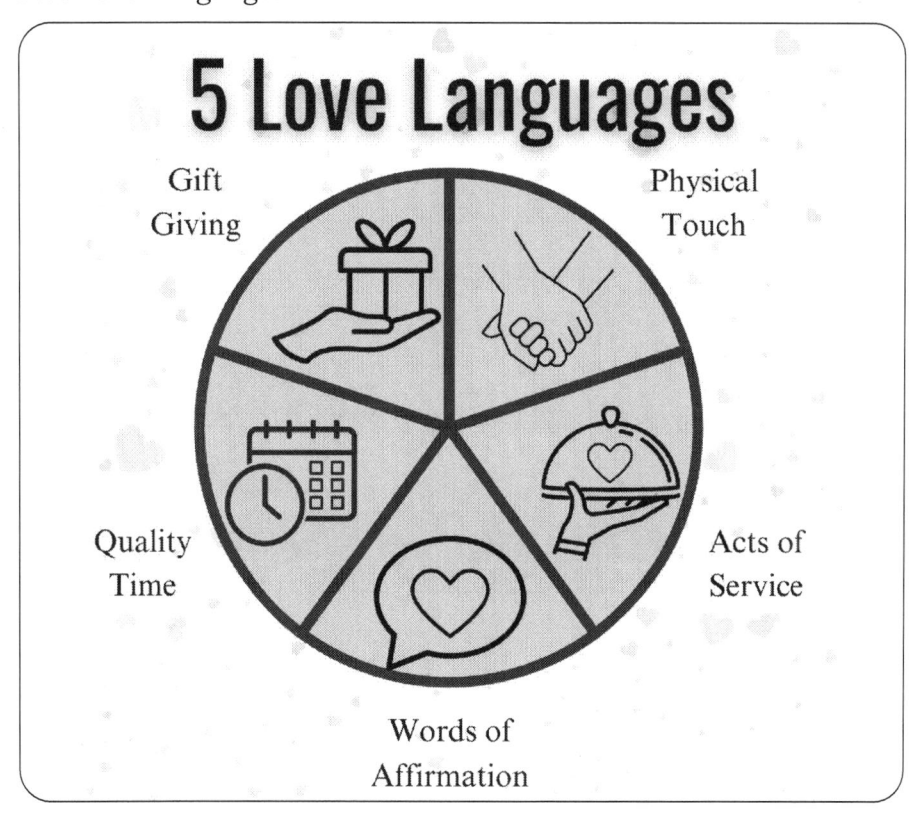

5 Love Languages

Gift Giving

Physical Touch

Quality Time

Acts of Service

Words of Affirmation

"Love is not something we give or get; it is something that we nurture and grow, a connection that can be cultivated between two people only when it exists within each of them–we can love others only as much as we love ourselves" (Brown, 2021, p.184).

> Gary Chapman's book, The Five Love Languages (1992), shares his five ideas for how people can give/receive love. If you were to consider these, what would be your love language, and why?

Hope-In-Action

Figure 9

Hope-In-Action Tool

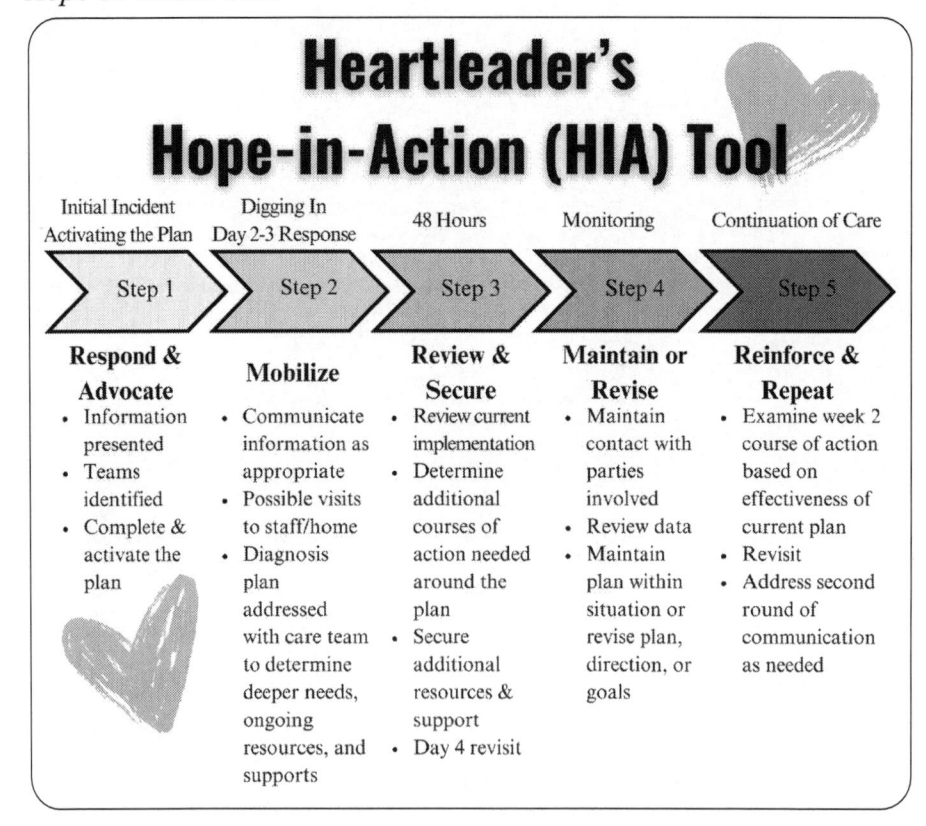

Heartleader's Hope-in-Action (HIA) Tool

Initial Incident Activating the Plan	Digging In Day 2-3 Response	48 Hours	Monitoring	Continuation of Care
Step 1	**Step 2**	**Step 3**	**Step 4**	**Step 5**
Respond & Advocate	**Mobilize**	**Review & Secure**	**Maintain or Revise**	**Reinforce & Repeat**
• Information presented • Teams identified • Complete & activate the plan	• Communicate information as appropriate • Possible visits to staff/home • Diagnosis plan addressed with care team to determine deeper needs, ongoing resources, and supports	• Review current implementation • Determine additional courses of action needed around the plan • Secure additional resources & support • Day 4 revisit	• Maintain contact with parties involved • Review data • Maintain plan within situation or revise plan, direction, or goals	• Examine week 2 course of action based on effectiveness of current plan • Revisit • Address second round of communication as needed

We are living in this time of tremendous love and hope that continues to survive and thrive in the face of our collective traumas. The Hope-in-Action (HIA) Tool is meant to be a proactive plan that exists in some form as part of your school improvement work. Family stakeholders with seats at your school improvement meetings will be able to recognize and implement this tool should the need arise in the community, just as staff would be aware of it as an operational resource in the school's Heartleading initiatives. It is designed, along with the previous flowchart, to support the focus person or group and participating team members throughout the event. While this can be adapted for any school community or need, the ones I have previously created were attached to family, student, staff, community need, and personal wellness.

There are many types of triggering events connected with heartache. You are probably all-too-familiar with some of these; perhaps you have experienced some of these first-hand.

- Ongoing emotional and physical toll of the pandemics of racial injustice and COVID.
- Poverty
- Financial challenges
- The loss of a spouse, family member, or significant other
- A breakup, separation, or divorce
- The loss of or death of a pet
- A move of residency
- A military deployment of a partner, family member, or friend

"Love should be defined by parties...sometimes someone may show love too fast, too much, which will be perceived as manipulation. It is extremely important to listen and encourage first so that love flows organically into the relationship, especially in a professional environment. For families, it takes time, involvement, and planning to ensure that you will be trusted enough for the family to accept love. It is also important to notice that love should be shared in genuine and culturally competent ways."
—Saida Hentati, Parent Community Coordinator, Maryland

- Social media including unfriending, blocking, harassment, information overload or other challenges related to social media or dating websites
- The loss of a job

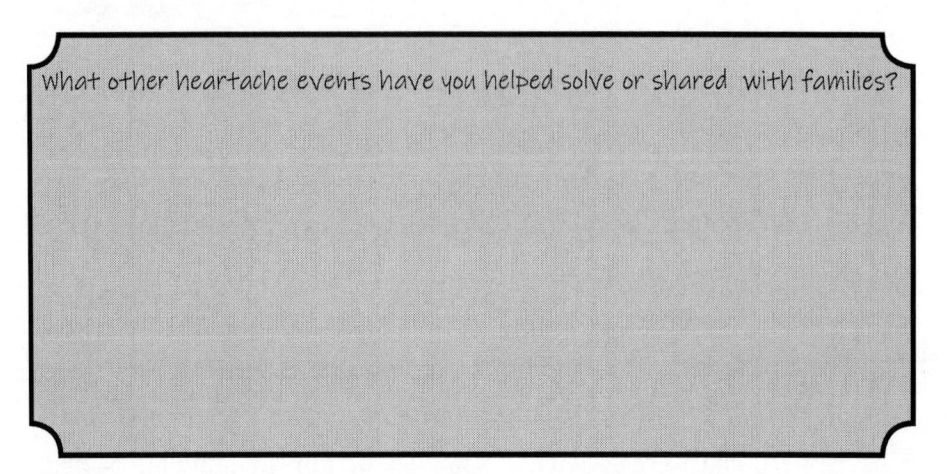

> What other heartache events have you helped solve or shared with families?

Heartleading Through Heartache

"When you lead with love and keep it real from that place of loving service to serve your staff, your students, families, everything else falls right into line, period. Things can get real hard along the way. You have to be able to lean into that, but love is what gets us to the right place, making our core values present, keeping true to who you are, and what you are about."

-Desmond Mackall, School Principal, BOND Educator

It is impossible to separate healing from loss, and just as people look to their trusted leaders when times are filled with hope so too will they reach for them in times of grief. The Heartleader in you addresses heartache with mindful listening, a calm and steady presence, and the ability to be authentically empathetic and compassionate. Your behavior is grounded in cultural competence because just as our love languages are different, so are the ways in which people process and deal with their grief, loss, and/or trauma. Sometimes being present is enough. Sometimes those in need want more or maybe less. Leading in love gives you just as much room to engage as it does to take a step back and give others space.

People who have experienced any of the heartaches we have been talking about don't just get over them. They don't go away. Through the love of friends or family, mental health supports, or other coping strategies people learn to live with and live through those things. I think eventually, with time and work, it becomes absorbed into the story. While not forgotten, it becomes a little less close to the skin, so to speak. It has for me over time, but it's never easy, and it never goes away.

It's important for Heartleaders who want to help, mend, and fix to also come to terms with the fact that we don't ever treat children or adults as broken, and not everyone wants someone else's help. As we've discussed, we are not their parents or caregivers, and boundaries must be respected, especially in this area of our work. Again, it's about building that competence for ourselves. Our outreach efforts and our communication won't always be able to patch things up for our students and families, and so we should be ready to just listen, offer safe space, while remaining present and emotionally available.

Heartache in all of its forms, especially in working with lives in trauma, is as complex as the people it affects. For example, it can be from a recent event, something several years old, or fragmented across generations, borne of intergenerational loss. Many times it can reoccur with those involved either directly or vicariously, caught in a continuing loop triggering those survivors, repeatedly.

> Trauma-affected children become finely tuned detectors of their environments. They constantly scan their environments for any tiny cue that would help them determine "I am safe" or "I am not safe," even if those cues seem insignificant to others…a trauma-affected child's brain says, "Better safe than sorry" and activates the stress-response system (Venet, 2021, p.35).

You cannot maneuver in the spaces of this work alone. You must be able to recognize the limitations of your role and prioritize collaboration with administration, peers, and other mental health practitioners. "Preservice training programs seldom prepare teachers for the effects of trauma and violence on children's learning and development. As a result, teachers are caught off guard by the life experiences of the children in their care" (Craig, 2008, p.164).

Keep in mind, however, you don't need to know all about someone's trauma to love them, or to be loving towards them. As we know, everyone's origin is different, and how they tell it, live it, and show it requires a unique kind of listening. Remember, no two stories are the same.

Consider some of the feedback school staff have shared with me in interviews just since 2012.

"I want to help, but I'm not really trained to deal with all of this."

"What can we really do to help with that much damage?"

"Is this something the school really expects me to take on?"

"What if I cause more harm?"

"Why do I feel so alone in trying to help this child?"

"What about what all of this does to me? Am I in danger?"

"The stories and the needs keep coming; it feels like it never never stops."

Intentionally engaging with your colleagues around the issues that affect them allows you to develop empathetic relationships with them. The extent of what you are able to give or share will depend on the feedback you receive from them about what they need or want from their workplace relationship with you. It is important to learn this with them openly and up front. The act of being available or providing space to listen can be some of your most restorative supports for them and, by extension, positively impact the broader school community.

It's clear that school staff have been through a lot, and despite the need to move forward in school systems, both nationally and internationally, this knowledge must be safeguarded. Their questions, their struggles, and their needs are your opportunity as a colleague. Choosing to provide assistance, to demonstrate some aspect of workplace-supported love towards another human being, especially in the day-to-day of school, is an active choice. There is nothing passive about giving love, especially when the act is grounded in self-

"To heal is to touch with love that which we previously touched with fear."
- Stephen Levine

lessness, knowing that there should be no expectation for if and when, or in what way, it is returned. Chapman (1992) has shared that for love it is about choices, and the choice to act; to do or say something that would help another person, that would be for their benefit, or make them a better person, or make life better for them.

Let's operationalize the love again; take a look at these scenarios, and consider your responses to the corresponding questions around the next steps.

Situation: A first-grade student is crying, tearing up paper, and using scissors to jab the underside of the desk while yelling, "No, no!" repeatedly. He has already thrown toys around the room from one of the discovery centers and is now under his desk. It is his first day at this school.

Heartleading Decision Making: How do you approach this as a Heartleader? How do you establish that next moment of communication? What do you need to consider about the staff and students in the room? Who else should join you to support?

Situation: A grade-level middle-school team is struggling to plan together. As a result, the data shows clear drops in student performance over two separate assessments. While class size and behavior seem to be stable overall, staff are struggling with new curriculum, aligning priorities, and onboarding new team members. You are a member of this team.

Heartleading Decision Making: What would your next step be in terms of Heartleading action to support the team's feelings? What does the data suggest about the delivery method of instruction, and how honest can the team get with themselves and one another? As a Heartleader, what do you think would unify this team?

Situation: You hear an argument outside of a classroom where you find an eleventh-grade male student pacing in a circle emphatically stating, "I just want my phone back." He is agitated and in an elevated emotional state. A staff member keeps pointing and repeating: "You want the phone back, you follow my rules. It is that simple." The staff member turns to you and says, "This is strike three. I just can't be with him anymore. You deal with him."

Heartleading Decision Making: What Heartleading move would support de-escalating this and eliminate the hallway visibility? What do you believe is happening here between the student and staff member? What is one error each is making that creates a blockage between them? What might an appropriate role be for you in this situation?

Situation: Two seventh-grade males were observed throwing mulch at a seventh-grade female student, insulting her, and teasing her in another language. She has an IEP and mobility needs. During the incident, she was crying and the males were following her around, pointing at her. At one point she turned and screamed at them. They surrounded her and became threatening. Two of her friends ran over and pushed the boys away.

Heartleading Decision Making: What is one of your first action steps in this situation around supporting a vulnerable student? What information do you need to fully explore this incident? Beyond this moment, how could you and the lunch-recess staff support all of these students?

Situation: You are on your way to a meeting when you see a ninth-grade student who identifies as female sitting on the floor, legs stretched out, up against the lockers in the hallway. It is the middle of third period. Her hood covers her head, a crushed-up water bottle set on the floor next to her along with a cellphone with a cracked screen. In her hands is a small multi-tool she is playing with, running a small blade across their fingers. When you approach they look up and say, "Can I help you? I'm busy plotting my death."

> **Heartleading Decision Making:** What might this student be feeling? What do you observe that leads you to that conclusion? What clues are apparent? What safety concerns are there?

Every scenario here presents an opportunity to create harm or remove it based entirely on whether we are responsive or reactive. Often we are catching these events with students, staff, or families as they are happening or after the initial antecedent for the incident making us purely reactive, but the majority of the work we build for communities should come from a place of prevention by responding to the formal and informal data that has been collected and prior to an incident. The goal is to have spaces, communication, and procedures that focus on being stewards in the school. This is to say our business is the people; we build up life in a school, we elevate inspiration, and design opportunities for students to be loved in ways that support their pain, their curiosity, their struggles, failures, and successes. We must envision school in a way that not only meets them where they are, but recognizes that where they are may be in places of extremely challenging personal need. We should have an environment, staffing, training, and a vision that is already built to serve in the most holistic ways possible.

Pursuing Balance

Most people know what they need to do to take care of themselves in one form or another, but getting it done with all we have to manage can feel downright impossible at times. "You know what makes you tick, what makes you happy, angry, sad...when you stop, listen, slow down, when you find balance, life is so much more beautiful" (Donald, personal communication, March 2021). First, give yourself permission to be human, right? We know it takes effort and consistent, hard work. Balance may feel intuitive, but it is not something we seem to consciously arrange in our daily lives as a species.

Prioritizing balance is really about understanding *homeostasis*. "It derives from the Greek words for 'same' and 'steady,' which refers to any process that living things use to actively maintain fairly stable conditions necessary for survival." (Rodolfo, 2020, para. 1).

For educators, there is balance when our systems function properly, and we have taken care to create stability, address our needs, and act 'homeostatically' in order to make sure the system (in this case us–our brain and body) are functioning properly and is at balance with itself. Without a sense of homeostasis, our natural balance is out of order. That is when physical illness, deteriorating job performance, relationship issues, and mental health challenges can rear their ugly head as a response to systems being out of flux. That's heavy science coming at us fast every day. Creating and maintaining balance is imperative for us to remain aligned with nature's own desire for how we operate as a complex system.

Additionally, making the personal investment in compassion and learning to become understanding of what everyone may be going through is important work. With this work that is difficult, messy, and beautiful, members of your staff might not yet be in a self-knowledge place, so meet them where they are with love, give them compassion, and give them understanding. You always play a part in helping others and sharing love.

The more we help one another, the more we connect and by extension take care of one another, which is a great way to support the health and wellness of our educational ecosystem. There may be those who interpret balance as an act of faith, tied to universal conditions around religious or spiritual figures that are prayed to in a search for a grounded position in the world. Some may see balance as a concept as old as the creation of the world, centered in the language of oneness where everything is connected and responsible for everything else. That balance is only achieved when all elements exist in place. Other people may see balance as simply paying the bills, owning a home and bank accounts, or enjoying a family meal without worrying about someone taking away a loved one. Their balance is security and peace of mind.

The Balance of Instruction

Within a school, one of the critical systems that must operate with a sense of homeostasis are instructional practices. The building is a vehicle for an operating system that is composed of thousands of moving parts, and those parts must work together to create, in essence, *homeostasis*, as a "stable state of equilibrium or a tendency toward such a state between the different but interdependent elements or groups of elements of an organism, population, or group that steady balance through which all things, together, work cohesively" (Merriam Webster, 2021).

Heartleaders help to engage the systems in ways that support operational efficiency and seek to maximize the efforts and output through many of the leadership moves explored throughout this book.

In terms of the systems that drive school success, Heartleaders are instructional coaches. They must bring love and a critical equity lens to pedagogy, content, and improving instruction. Heartleaders in every role participate in decision-making that supports conversation and action around what functional instructional programs must look like.

Those who hold leadership roles provide the observations and evaluations that build teacher and staff capacity with actionable feedback; it is important to note that the majority of roles in schools are not supervisory, and therefore not directly involved in evaluating staff. Heartleaders, in many capacities in a school, can collaborate with teachers, internal school leaders (department chairs, team leaders, instructional coaches, etc.), and administration in order to build the protocols necessary to collect and analyze data.

From this approach, one can assess baselines and identify areas of strength and growth with short and long-term goals. This is especially true as it applies to marginalized communities, special needs populations, and students who are new to the American educational system or whose native language is not English.

I have leaned into the discomfort that my personal learning needs created as both a child and adult and prioritized this instructional role and the learning it requires of me into a weekly practice of self-reflection, conversations with other experts, and specific action when I work with staff. Data tells a powerful story and provides its own undeniable origin of what a school speaks to when examining its past, present, and future. For example, when you think about your role in the school improvement process and how you use data, what do the conversations around data look like in your school communitywide and at the micro-levels? How often do these conversations take place related to data and school improvement? In what ways is data collected by grade levels? Consider the questions in the following graphic as part of the heart of your data story.

Figure 10

Your School's Data Story

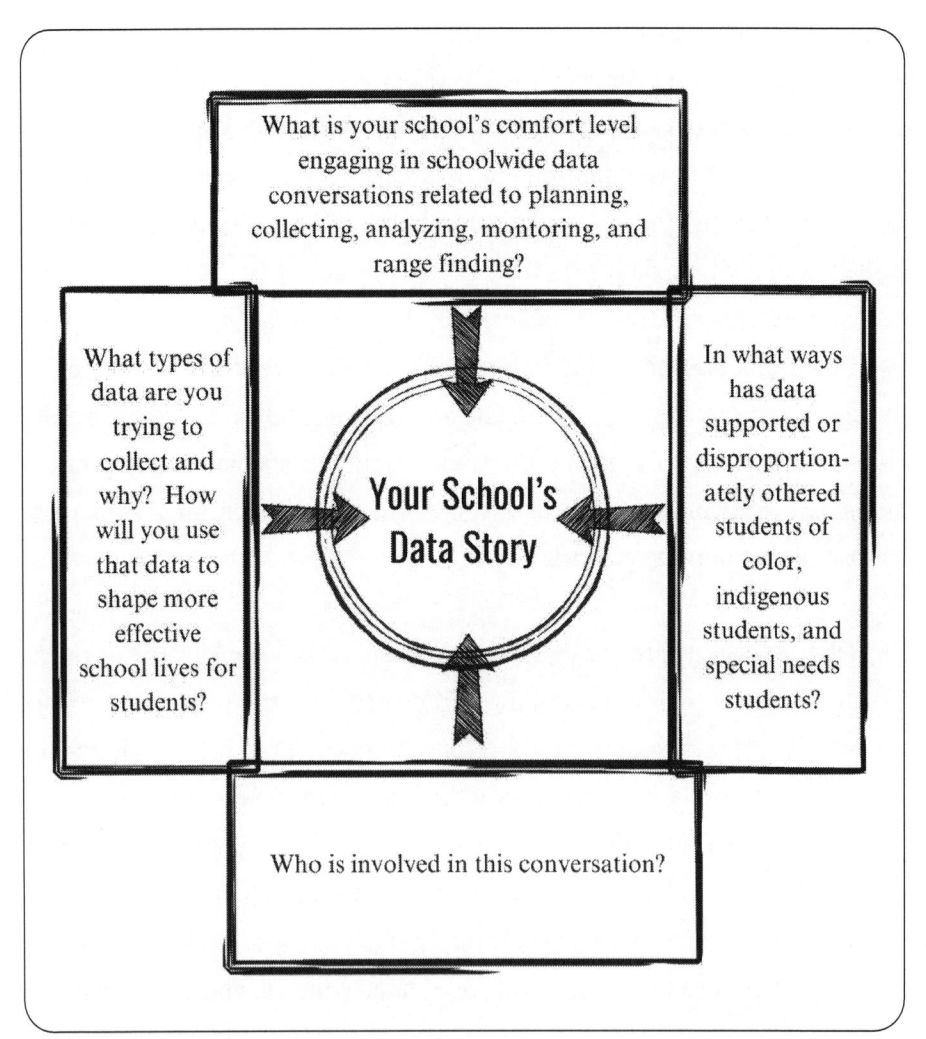

- What is your school's comfort level engaging in schoolwide data conversations related to planning, collecting, analyzing, montoring, and range finding?
- What types of data are you trying to collect and why? How will you use that data to shape more effective school lives for students?
- In what ways has data supported or disproportionately othered students of color, indigenous students, and special needs students?
- Who is involved in this conversation?

Your School's Data Story

The following QR code takes you to one sample of an alternative data collection tool that captures data a Heartleader would use to examine the aperture of a school, review its culture and climate, observe equitable practices, and determine the nature of the relationship language and behaviors demonstrated between students and adults.

The emotional pain that comes with working closely with trauma and the challenge of infusing such a deeply impactful emotion (love) into your daily work requires time to grasp and likely even more time to figure out how to maintain a balance. Relationships take time to develop, and adaptive challenges will always be something educators are tasked with overcoming in school communities. Instructional coaching, relationship-building, and consistently challenging your own practices from a wide and culturally competent emotional aperture are the daily menu. I continue to find that there is always something pressing around the corner for those engaged in our work. Being a leader is not defined by the position title but by the work you do and your impact on others. 'Typical' or technical challenges constitute those situations where the normal tools, protocols, and policies of leadership can be used to affect change and solve a given challenge.

Adaptive challenges break from the norm and require, often improvisationally at first, a whole new set of rules and tools being developed around some considerable, flexible thinking. In this journey, we return to healing and trauma. Both converge in media centers, offices, hallways, playgrounds, lunchrooms, break rooms, and classrooms across this country. I created the R.E.S.T.O.R.E. approach to frame Heartleader moves that can be practiced every day and shared with your community as a quick, one-stop-shop view of how you will work with them.

The Restore Approach

- **Relationships** must be equitably cultivated between students and adults.
- **Extend** yourself to your students and their families always.
- **Share** feelings and thoughts about academics, behavior, and school needs in collaborative, transparent, authentic ways with your partners.
- **Trust** should be built with clearly defined boundaries in both directions.
- **One** moment, one child, one family at a time.
- **Responsibility** is built on personal and communal accountability and connected with allyship, and geared towards open dialogue and healing.
- **Examine** and eliminate implicit and explicit biases within yourself, through others, and around the system.

Our communities have been listening, and they want to speak. They want to share in the hopes that they will be seen and that their voices will be heard. Let's be the leaders they deserve in the schools and communities.

Figure 11
R.E.S.T.O.R.E.

R elationships
E xtend
S hare
T rust
O ne
R esponsibility
E xamine

> If you're reading this, you are someone who believes or is learning to believe in the power of love and Heartleading for student success and family engagement. What is something in your work that has shaped you to want to lead with this as your focus?

Learn Your Audience and Create Space

School communities have neighborhoods, and those neighborhoods have history and residents invested in the welfare of the spaces they call home. If you want to be effective in creating trust and developing genuine relationships, you must learn about your community and its beliefs. Khalifa (2018) states:

> ... that by learning about and embracing community interests, and by humanizing students in school, eductors can contribute to student achievement…they establish trusting relationships that are needed if students decide to stay and learn from them; they gain the support of community elders and learn what is important to them and their collective aspirations. Educators affirm student identify by having people from their communities in school. Educators and school leaders will then begin to be embraced by communities in school, and this rapport is grounded in trust (p.175).

In designing intentional outreach, does your school have a parent organization that is embedded in the pulse of the school? If so, are they representative of the community you serve, and if not, how can outreach be shaped to correct this? What is the history of their dynamic with school administration and local community partners? These types of groups can potentially bring considerable cultural awareness, expertise, and knowledge to the conversations of relationship-building, again, a fundamental element of school improvement. When we talk school improvement and our parent organizations, it relates directly to their ability to elevate communication of critical school messaging, provide access to resources and funding, support the instructional and social-emotional programs of the school, and coordinate with school staff to serve as a proverbial bridge between all of the families and the school leadership.

Heartleaders are present at those meetings and make it a priority to connect with those parents with the intent of partnering to support the community in a way that pulls back the curtain and makes thinking and action transparent. That work extends beyond the monthly meeting or lone school event and must be centered in equitable, sustainable practices that speak to a desire to include community voice at every level of a school and use that voice to shape improvement. From a culturally responsive lens, one relationship building example of this would be communicating with communities and their leaders that you would like to come join them in fellowship, seeking permission to enter their neighborhoods in a sense, adding translators as needed to your team, and going directly into those communities (local town hall, place of worship, community park or playground) to share your face, your voice, and your love for the place and people you seek to serve.

Spaces to meet should be flexible and supportive of the needs of your community. Creating an audit of past and/or current practices for these meetings will help to determine what has or has not worked. Families connect in different ways and having virtual meetings that are recorded with an in-person option, at times with translators or interpreters, would allow for the content to be shared digitally such as on the school website for people unable to attend. This approach thinks about families in a flexible way, understanding that work schedules and lives are not all the same. While parents and caregivers wish to know what is happening at school, they do not always have the time, means, or access to attending these meetings. It is imperative to make it as simple as possible for them to have the information and updates they need, when they need them. Remember, everyone deserves the chance to build up the school and show the community how they are willing and able to demonstrate their love.

To highlight a sample of bridge-building in the community and shaping action around the goal of community unity, here is the QR code to access the Heartleader Community Bridge-Builder and Sample Community Event Planner.

In addition, there is a follow-up response section for when challenges arise during the bridge-building work. Also, remember to adhere to the policies and protocols your school system may have in place for emergency response and community outreach. Their personnel, insights, and resources can only uplift the school-based response. As we know, this type of work is often fluid and emotionally charged. There are many nuances and high-stakes questions to support during emergent situations in a community.

Heartleaders bridge-build, and that work takes place on the ground, being with people, listening to their thoughts and ideas, and putting your face in front of them with the intent to connect and support. Here is some reflective homework for you, your teams, and school as you get your time, tools, and walking shoes organized.

- Define for yourself where you see yourself as a partnering unifier, as a commUNITY advocate, and what this work asks of you daily.

- Create a beginning. When appropriate and safe, visit neighborhoods with local families and community representatives. Take a tour with a local expert. Take staff on bus tours of the local routes, check out the parks, playgrounds, businesses, talk to people, and learn about them and know their stories.

- Communicate to families in their native language that you are going to be reaching out with an ask. Create a Google survey for families in order to prepare for the events. Make home visits to speak with families in order to gain perspective.

As we dig deeper into bridge-building and creating sustainable connections with a community, I think about words like conversation, dialogue, interaction, and inquiry. In my relationship-building with families of color, I have learned through their stories that inquiry often equals investigation, which historically has led to bullying and harassment, physical attacks, foreclosures on homes, loss of employment, home raids, and a host of other violences perpetrated on communities of color.

First, I find a way to take a step. A way to make contact, an introduction, and ask to visit or meet at a local park or playground. I create an opportunity and work to meet families where they are. Sometimes it happens naturally, like in a car rider line or at the grocery store, and sometimes it requires a different type of approach based on what the family needs.

I learned early on in conducting my home visits that often families of color and indigenous families do not necessarily want to be asked questions about how they feel about school, how race issues are affecting them, or what they think about their child's school experience. If one thing misappropriated history has taught them is that giving responses to questions, especially to caucasian people, can negatively affect their lives, and the lives of their children.

Much of this same insensitivity, violence, and miseducation has also been directed at our LGBTQIA+ populations. These are perceptions I have found many carry about inquiry and with good reason. This is one of the truths of our world and its public education systems. Interrogation has often bred suspicion, violence, and continued marginalization of communities already facing discrimination and oppression.

So I start simply with a beginning introduction and partner myself in ways that bring us together to start a conversation about how I can support them and what a teacher/leader looks, sounds, and feels like to them. What does love do about this? Safir and Dugan (2021) pull no punches when getting right to it:

> Our intentions may be spot-on, but if we aren't aware of the moves we are making, we are liable to reinforce the system we seek to dismantle. There are no shortcuts when it comes to leading for equity. If we hope to transform our institutions into vibrant spaces of learning for every student, we must revisit the fundamental purpose of education and commit to a long-term change process (p. 44).

How can Heartleading step into this place and time of history, avoid the surface approaches to equity work, and confront the oppressive nature of what permeates our history, and embrace systemic change? This is a question that must stand firm at the doorway of every meeting, at the opening of any conversation where staff and students are the subject.

Heartleaders must engage with many people in this race and equity work, and not step into it without an open-minded understanding of what is being done, why it is being done, and what type of impact is being sought from the change. This work must be built in tandem with those who have been marginalized, and those who have identified as allies. This has proven to be a highly visible part of the work for me, especially as a white, male leader, who seeks to engage as an ally, while consistently confronting my own story and privilege. "Equity isn't a destination but an unwavering commitment to a journey. It can be easy to focus on where we hope to land and lose sight of the deliberate *daily* actions that constitute the process" (Safir & Dugan, 2021, p.29).

It's not easy to confront a system that has caused so much harm, but our society and schools are heading in a direction that calls for Heartleaders to step forward. They need to help train staff, improve students' understanding of different cultures, and work closely with families. This way, the approach becomes more genuine and inclusive.

Essentially, we are building out our stories when we use this approach, and it is a non-negotiable step in revisioning our current and future efforts. Creating a system that recognizes past wrongs and uses them to nurture a narrative of diversity in every school and community is important. This system should ensure that everyone has equal access to education and opportunities, and Heartleaders should guide students, families, and staff in practicing fairness, sustainability, and anti-racism. "Only by abolishing the situations of oppression is it possible to restore the love which that situation made impossible. If I do not love the world—if I do not love life—if I do not love—I cannot enter into dialogue" (Friere, 1970, p.90). Consider these voices in leading this work forward, and think about what resonates with you in their statements from their experiences in school communities.

> Being 'included' in a system that was not designed for your family's goals and edification is not a gift,' says Jennifer Malone, PTO co-president at Longfellow Elementary in Oak Park, Illinois. 'Be sure you ask what your Black and Brown families want to see and need to see change. Just inviting is not necessarily welcoming. People who are disenfranchised are not going to just show up unless they believe they will actually get a seat at the table (Leaver, 2021, para. 5).

> Despite progress, unwelcoming school climates continue to take a toll on the well-being of LGBTQ students (Sadowski, 2016, pg.6).

> Trust is built over time, based on interactions that occur on a daily basis and with consistent behavior from both sides. If the families and educators do not have experience interacting with one another, then they may rely on the other person's reputation and on something they have in common, such as race, gender, age, religion, or upbringing (Bryk & Schneider, 2002, as referenced in Garcia et. al, 2016). When there are few things in common between families and educators, it will take time for trust to develop. The willingness to trust each other will be based on actions and perceptions

of each other's reliability, competence, honesty, and openness (Garcia, et. al, 2016, p.6).

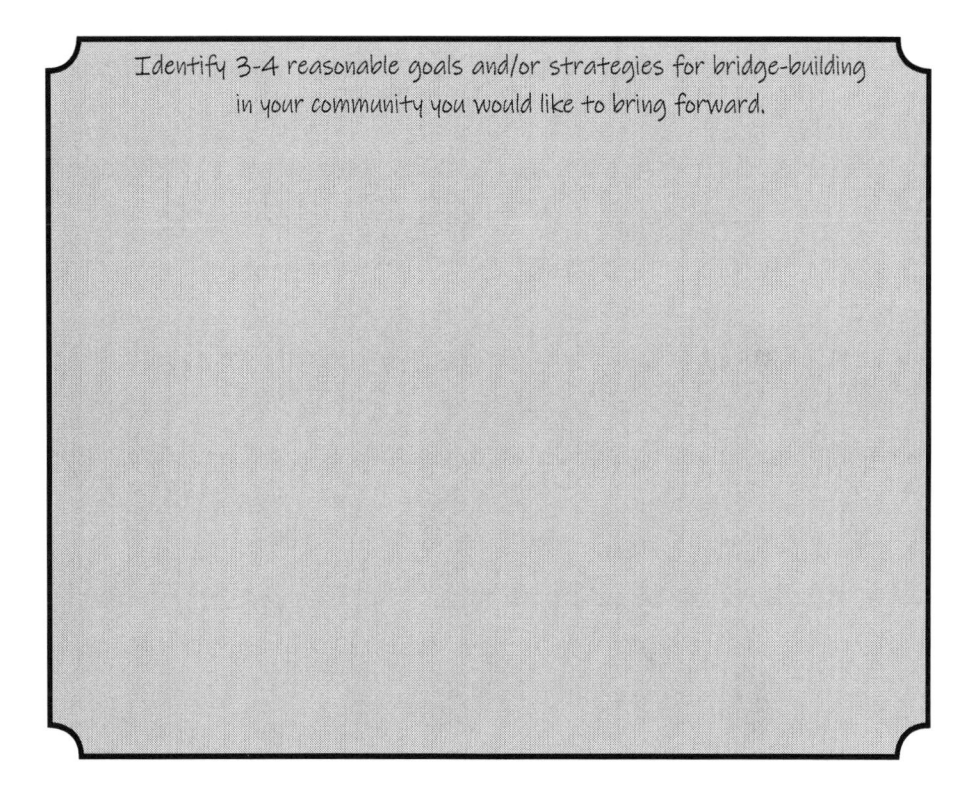

> Identify 3-4 reasonable goals and/or strategies for bridge-building in your community you would like to bring forward.

HEARTBEATS

Heartleading uplifts hope, but there will always be elements of struggle, trauma, and loss connected with the work.

- Heartache is real with long-lasting effects. Grieving often takes as much time as healing.
- We cannot think we understand every aspect of someone else's ex-

perience with trauma and/or struggle, but we can always work on knowing our own and provide safe space to learn from those we work with and serve.
- Practice creating and maintaining safe, healthy boundaries that safeguard you, your role, and those you work with. When in doubt, ask for help.
- Explore your love language(s), and make it part of your Heartleading to support learning other's love languages in the workplace.
- Bridge building can always get you there in supporting engagement work with families. Prioritize a Hope-In-Action Plan.
- You don't need to know someone else's trauma to love them.
- Always keep race on the table. Teaching and leading for equity must be a defining lens by which to engage in every conversation about school improvement. Love leads us to disrupt and dismantle inequity and racism at all costs.
- In what ways can you promote R.E.S.T.O.R.E in your school role?
- Compassion fatigue is a legitimate concern, so you must have support measures in place for your staff.
- There is nothing passive about giving love to those we serve.
- Building your mental health and balance is critical to supporting that work in others.
- Being a leader has never been defined by position or title, but by actions and impact. Let's be the educators, the leaders, that our communities deserve.

10. The Ones Who Know

"Love in action is service to the world."

-Dr. Lynne Namka, Licensed Psychologist

The ones who know are the ones who do. I cannot tell you exactly where I was when I heard this for the first time, but in my years spent teaching, researching, and ultimately writing this book, I have come into contact with a vast amount of non-educators who believe in the inherent power that educators have to shape the world. From my many years of interviews and research, I have experienced countless school staff, students, and parents who have given me hope and consistently reinforced my belief in the work that we do. I learned this from those teachers who shaped my life course; where there is a need, you just do. When you want to do good, you do. The ones who know this are never passive in their doing; they are proactive, responsive, and consistently doing. I've always told my children, "We do the right thing in the world because it's the right thing to do." Along the way, I have tried to give them the skills to recognize and pursue the right things in the world, and that the love we can offer is also equal to the acts of goodness we can do for others.

The ones who do–what do they really know, and where did they learn it? Why are they driven to do, to operate at that level of involvement with people and situations? Does it require a certain level of passion, skill, or instinct? How long did it take them to learn what they know, and is it teachable? As a person who considers themself to be a doer, I can answer that question. It is teachable, as much as love is something to be given to others. You can guide and empower others to seek out opportunities to act simply because it is in the best interest of improving a person or a school. Do I have all the answers? Not even close. Most days I go to bed with far more questions than answers, but I do keep asking because that practice of inquiry helps to inform my mental health work, my school improvement planning, and just about all of my decision-making. It helps keep me on my toes from an accountability standpoint and I try to ask difficult questions of myself. Engaging in that behavior consistently pushes me to consider my behavior, as well as possible solutions to areas of myself that ask for improvement. They are my '6 to Fix'--six questions to challenge and ground me. In order to sharpen my leadership skills, as well as my overall people skills, here is language framing around things I am currently working on repairing in my life. Maybe they can help your reflections.

I start like this...*Matthew, take a breath. (I usually do five deep ones.) Tomorrow you start again; tonight you question as a way to prepare for again. You made a lot of decisions today and came in contact with a lot of people. Were you the best husband, father, educator, and person you could be? What was today's story?*

- What's one situation or decision you are trying to work through? Where do you feel it in your body, and why do you think that?

- Did making that decision fill, feed, or fix something for you?
- Are you a better person for doing that, or was it a decision that reversed the course of your love?
- What motivated you–pride, ego, selfishness, rage, fear, insecurity, humiliation?
- What harm(s) do you need to repair as a result of your behavior?
- What's one decision you made today that supported your growth and overall (mental/physical) health?

I have been fortunate to collaborate with many leaders of all types in the creation of this book. Here are some of their defining types and the core truths, ideas, and concepts they want all of us to consider in our personal and/or professional practices. We have each probably moved between some of these types before in both our personal and professional lives. We can evolve, occupying elements from more than one type. These leaders who have shared with us stepped right in with their hearts in the game everyday. They are military veterans, superintendents, freshly-minted principals, long-time stewards of multiple national and international counties and districts, CEOs, CFOs, area directors, and behind-the-scenes data gurus.

First and foremost, they are educators. Use the QR code to access the Leadership Inventory they would like you to enjoy!

> Which leadership types did you identify with from the inventory? How do you know?

I began with my origin; I am passionate about building relationships with staff by learning about theirs. I prize student engagement, academics, and social-emotional wellness by empowering children's stories as part of my everyday practices. I prioritize parents' lives by connecting to their experiences in order to determine how my role and my origin can align with theirs by supporting the amplification of their needs in the areas that are within my control.

As none of this work, including the shaping of myself, exists in a vacuum, I am empowered and encouraged by the origins and insights of others who do. Those who stand on the frontlines of love leadership and are Heartleaders in their own rights. I want to do better and be better in all of my practices. In examining how I can continue to do that, I reflected on those who have inspired my process. I have decided to feature four Heartleading colleagues in my school system who have had a considerable impact and whose beautiful origins and tremendous leadership can inspire us and further light the way for everyone's stories to be seen and heard. There are many others highlighted throughout this book, but I have observed these leaders, learned from them, and, most importantly, loved them as I have worked to model myself on how they work.

Four Different Heartleaders, Four Different Origins

Rajeev Gupta, Principal Intern

Rajeev Gupta is a second-generation immigrant from a tight-knit Indian family in suburban Washington, D.C. that places the greatest value on education. Rajeev's mother was the only person of color who graduated from Lakewood High School outside of Cleveland, Ohio in the late 1960s. Rajeev grew up in a much more diverse community in Gaithersburg, Maryland and graduated from Gaithersburg High School in 2001. After spending several years serving as an educational leader in the Las Vegas metropolitan area, he relocated back to Montgomery County, MD and Montgomery County Public Schools (MCPS) due to its emphasis on education, fostering multiculturalism and diversity, and building strong families and communities. Rajeev is married, and the father of three, amazing girls.

"I am a son of immigrant parents who did not complete education beyond community college."

His involvement in promoting equitable and enriching opportunities for all students also extended to numerous sports and extracurricular clubs including varsity golf, UNICEF, and MCPS Study Circles. Raj created and implemented the first-ever accounting program completer at his school. Of the first 20 graduates, 24% of this cohort had IEPs or 504s.

"I have a chance to welcome these students, many of whom are minority and immigrant children much like myself, to their school while serving as a constant reminder that they belong here, and that they will succeed. We operationalize love through action."

Rajeev worked for five years at Title I schools within the Clark County School District in inner-city, Las Vegas, NV. As per the information provided by the U.S. Department of Education in 2018, Title I is characterized by Part A (Title I) of the Elementary and Secondary Education Act, which has been modified by the Every Student Succeeds Act (ESEA). This initiative offers monetary support to local educational agencies (LEAs) and schools that serve a significant proportion of children from low-income families. The aim is to assist in guaranteeing that all children can achieve the demanding academic benchmarks set by their state. The district he was in is the fifth-largest school district in the United States and one of the lowest performing. Four of these five years were spent at Canyon Springs High School. In 2015, prior to his departure, he managed two major intervention programs which ultimately increased graduation rate percentages from 48% to 66%, the second highest gains in the state (Gupta, personal communication, June 2021). The expulsion rate also reduced from 186 students to 68 per year, the greatest decrease in Nevada.

"My familial core values and Indian heritage have shaped my vision in serving those around me. I understand the immense challenges of assimilation while trying to preserve my cultural and racial identities. I know what it feels like to be marginalized and not accepted; and through some of these personal, traumatic experiences, I have gained a powerful lens to lead by and not to do unto others what has been done to me."

Rajeev has engaged with many challenges as a leader who prioritizes both instruction and the social-emotional lives of his students. Getting into a groove during his first year as an elementary assistant principal, Rajeev found that the instructional constraints and trauma of the pandemic would push his leadership abilities to their limit.

"Over the next year or so, I helped implement a robust online learning program for about 500 students (grades 3-5). Further, I collaborated with central office partners to maintain parallel approaches between the 15th largest school district in our country and my small elementary school. I sought innovative ways to engage all our students to participate in learning, and helped as much as possible to build the capacities of our teachers and support staff. After the teaching and learning practices were ironed out, student well-being came to the forefront of our minds."

Rajeev's years as a leader are evident through his impact on school communities. Always reflective and culturally competent with an open heart and flexible mindset, Rajeev

> "Leadership is not about being in charge. It's about taking care of those in your charge."
> – Simon Sinek

reflected on two leadership moments that have informed his practices.

"I have prioritized anti-racist professional development stemming from a survey given to students, staff, and community members; there were several common themes. We worked in our leadership team to identify the priority areas to ensure our school feels welcome and inclusive to everyone. We created several days of professional development and accompanying content that examined our practices and how we could improve our teaching and learning practices for all students."

"I started a Boys 2 Men Club. In our national public education landscape, we often see historically underrepresented and marginalized student groups fall further behind white counterparts. As a 2nd generation immigrant, and one who struggled with my own Indian cultural identity and hardships in assimilation, I knew I could relate to our black and brown boys who felt as I did in my youth."

"I started a club to listen to and mentor this student group. I created a space during lunch and recess where I would meet with about a dozen students throughout the school year. We would openly speak about individual challenges but also discuss conflict resolution strategies, de-escalation techniques, problem-solving, race-related issues, and our greatest aspirations, fears, or ambitions. These students drastically improved in school. When I gave the students a survey, all students reported: 'a greater sense of belonging and purpose in school, a trusted adult that they could go to, improved attendance, and fewer disciplinary incidents.' On a few occasions, I reached out to their respective families and learned that the students shared positive experiences at home with the Boys 2 Men Club and looked forward to future meetings."

Rajeev is the quintessential gentleman as well as an avid golfer, golf coach, and former educational representative at the state and federal levels. As an athlete and statesman, his beliefs in professionalism, honesty, hard work, positive relationships, and mental discipline have smoothly transitioned into his caretaking for students and his high expectations for rigor in the classroom and academic excellence from every child, every day. He is also a talented gardener and is known for providing friends, family, colleagues, and staff with gifts of plants as a symbol of care, growth, and hope.

"I believe to be a steward for others means to celebrate their beautiful differences, to provide love and care as main ingredients to social emotional learning, and to never think you are above anyone else...I try to make others feel loved and included; I try to ensure that everyone has a place in my school and a voice in it...so to lead with love means to show love. This is the only way to combat hatred and/or injustices...to inspire a better future for those oftentimes marginalized students, and for all children really, is to unite our communities through love."

Saanura James, Assistant Principal

"I'm a Black woman of West Indian descent, raised by my white, German nanny in England... our caregivers' stories impact our stories tremendously."

Saanura was born in Hounslow, England and raised by her nanny from six weeks old to seven years of age. She would go home on the weekends, to see her biological parents and spend time with them, but she called her nanny 'mummy' because she thought she was her mother, and her nanny called Saanura 'her daughter' because that was how she was treated. That was primarily all Saanura had known. Her nanny breathed into her a lot of confidence, and she was the one who first told Saanura she was a leader.

"My nanny told me one day after an incident with some children, 'Well, you're a leader Jayne. You get out there and show them how it's supposed to be done.' She poured positivity, and unconditional love into me. She started me on my path to where I am now."

Jayne is Saanura's middle name and the only name she was called while growing up in England. It wasn't until her University years that she would take on her first name. She is one of six children between her biological parents. She is, in her words, a true daddy's girl. Her birth mother is from Trinidad and Tobago, and her father was from Montserrat. Her weekday life and weekend life was very different. One Easter Sunday, her father and mother got into a quarrel over whether or not she could stay at her nanny's house after dinner with her parents.

Her mother won the quarrel, and the next day she was awoken by her biological mother and asked if she would like to go to America. Jayne replied, "Oh yes that's where Mickey Mouse lives. Is daddy coming?" Her mother's answer was no. The next thing she knew, her bags were packed and she, her sisters, and her biological mother were on a plane to the United States. She found herself in Brooklyn, New York without her nanny's love and comfort and without her father's consent or approval. They were gone. Her life in England ended; her life in the

United States was just beginning.

"I know what true love feels like, and I know what it feels like to have it torn from you...I understand feelings of abandonment. I've survived that trauma. I know what it feels like to be a child from a different place coming to an unfamiliar country; I understand how to empathize with that because I was that child; I've experienced that. I want my students to know they belong."

In the summer of 1979 in Brooklyn, New York, the 7-year-old from England struggled to find her place in a new world. School was her only familiar place; she always loved school. While so much felt strange, school was something she could connect to. She was good at school academically, excelled at connecting with people, and her West Indian parents were very clear that school and proper education were the priority full stop. Her old life was over, and she had to figure out her new way.

"I want the kids leaving school each day wanting to come back. I strive to know 'what do we need to do to make them look forward to returning to school the next day?' They have no choice, right? They have to be here every day, so they should experience some measure of success, and a desire to return, to be in this place. Part of my work is helping them to find that place in themselves, and here in this building."

Saanura, like many children of West Indian parentage, continued on her path of scholarship and success. Her education was her focus. Her father dictated her academic path and higher education direction. It was during her junior year at college that she boldly left the path of entrepreneurship that her father had set and pursued her passion for teaching.

She earned a Bachelor of Science in Early Childhood Education from Temple University, a Master Certification in Technology Education and Leadership from Johns Hopkins University, and finally, a Master of Arts in Administration from Grand Canyon University. This is her 25th year in the field that she loves.

"Really speaking to children in the building, observing them, knowing if they are satisfied, safe, comfortable, and then dissecting what the next steps are for student and school improvement--not being too hasty, really listening to the children and looking...this is what I believe in, and this is what the leaders I have encountered in all of my schools who have made the most impact have done."

Saanura was the only black educator in her school during her first year in Montgomery County Public Schools. Fun fact: she is currently one of three in her current school.

"As I work with my students, I pray and think about what words each child needs to hear. What seeds do I need to plant? Because with our words, we can plant seeds of doubt, anxiety, or self- hatred, or we can plant seeds of courage, of hope, of love. We can plant the seeds that change them. I share this truth about the power of words with my students' caregivers. We must be careful with what words we plant in our children. Those seeds grow and impact who they can be."

Saanura's leadership style that she embraces in her love-leading is built on the knowledge that education is the prize. Heartleaders are truly aware of the impact they have on the spaces they are in. They are selfless; they possess a servant's heart; they understand that they won't get recognition for everything they do. In fact, they are not motivated by that recognition. We do this work in service of the students. We willingly pour in more than what is needed because that is what this role asks of us.

Saanura lives grounded in her faith and cultivates an attitude of gratitude, living out a daily belief that she has been called to do this work. She is grateful for the opportunity to give back, guide students, and provide them a safe and consistent place to grow both socially and academically.

"You are in school to get an education, but if you cannot access that experience because of certain feelings, it is my job to help determine what tools you need so that you can get your education...education is your prize to earn, to achieve; so how can we get elementary kids to know that their education is their prize? We have to first teach them the social-emotional skills to work through their day, it has to be taught. That's where we start, and from there we work our way to the prize."

Having held multiple leadership positions, Saanura has learned to navigate the dynamics of relationships, the power of persistence, and the belief that student success comes from transparent, consistent collaboration. Saanura shared two insights about leading during times of adaptive change by exposing instructional gaps and creating partnerships to do what is best for students.

"It was my first year as an administrator at the elementary school level. We completed our school improvement goals, and we began to work towards them. In mid-September, the new English for Speakers of Other

Languages (ESOL) team leader approached me. She was worried about the direction of the work for our multilingual learners. Together we analyzed the data from the ACCESS for English Language Learners (ELL) assessment and saw disparities in the areas of speaking and writing for our students. Thankfully, I worked for a principal that allowed me to take risks as a leader. She gave us the green light to develop a plan around student-to-student discourse techniques and writing scaffolds to support our students. After reviewing our plan, my principal went a step further and folded our action plan into the school improvement plan (SIP). She gave us room to audit our ESOL/Emerging Multilingual Learners (EML) department, infuse those language teachers as leaders in the planning process, and adopted a professional learning progression for teachers around the discourse strategies and writing scaffolds to be utilized with all students. In one year we changed outcomes for our English Language Learners, not only on the WIDA ACCESS test, but as members of the classroom community. Our voice data revealed that our children said they felt seen, they got help with their school work, and they made friends. I learned not to let opportunities for student progress slip through our fingers. We could have waited for the next school year. The SIP plan was done, but the work for the students would have been incomplete. My principal allowed me to lead for all students. They all matter, and we must seize the moments to move them forward."

"I had the honor of being a Science Content Specialist at the middle school level. I have always been the type of leader who believes in the potential of circumstances and people. I was determined to bring the department together. In three years as the department head, I led the mission for excellence in STEM (Science, Technology, Engineering, and Math) instruction. I ordered every material necessary to create a pro-

gram for students that included weekly cooperative, hands-on learning experiences. I challenged my teachers to work together as we analyzed and improved our teaching which translated into elevating our students academically. Each year we saw growth on our 8th grade Maryland Integrated Science Assessments (MISA) scores. We taught our children how to study. We encouraged creativity, curiosity, and thinking. We ended the science is hard myth and replaced it with the science is everywhere reality. My motto was, 'Make sure that they can't wait to come back to your class tomorrow.' We began the annual Science Extravaganza Event which was led by the students' research. I remember the first year. Every student presented on that night. They created models, board displays, and sold their work to the community members. Our students demonstrated deep knowledge about biology, chemistry, earth space science, environmental problems, and solutions. Leading that department was one of the highlights of my career. Our efforts showed up in the work of the children."

Always a loving person with a mission to bring kindness, clarity, and support to every interaction, Saanura is a natural-born leader, and sums up the work of a Heartleader with this:

"Heartleading is selflessness; you have opportunities to really change things for teachers you lead and students that you serve in a positive direction through their academic and their social-emotional awareness, being available when you enter the building, to hear and learn from what they have to say--the people you serve are the people who help you lead that work."

Norka Padilla, Instructional Specialist with International Admissions and Enrollment/Student Family Support and Services

"Love is the center of everything. Love is a verb; it's an action. If we want our children, teachers, leaders, families, and communities to change, to learn, we can and will find ways to do so lovingly."

Norka Padilla was born in Washington, D.C. and raised trilingual by her Guatemalan father and Norwegian mother. After moving to Maryland in middle school, she was "othered" into an English for Speakers of Other Languages class, inspiring her early on to seek a career in educational reform.

Her journey included teaching children and their caregivers from all over the world, including preliterate refugees of war in dire circumstances.

"I personally think it is very important to never forget why we do what we do. Our children, families, and communities are at the center of our work, our service. We serve with our students, with our families, and with our community. We are building our futures together, invested in our collective trajectory...and ensuring every space is psychologically safe so that when we lean in for equity and intellectually stimulating learning that relies on meeting high expectations that every learner, whether adult or child, can engage with their appreciated authentic selves."

Norka collaborates with her educational partners locally, nationally, and internationally to ensure children have equitable access to high-quality, standards-aligned first instruction. She supports a team in service with schools, community partners, mental health professionals, and families. Norka has over 30 years of experience as a K-12 teacher and an instructional specialist for curriculum and school improvement.

"A Heartleader serves, and they serve with inspiration, positivity, modeling, truth, authenticity, openness, competency, cultural responsiveness, and in comforting and bold ways with integrity. They walk the talk, and have a 'do whatever it takes' attitude with care, and ensures that we serve everyone, meeting them where they are non-judgmentally, demonstrating competence in practices, knowledgeable, and wise."

When asked about creating safe spaces to do difficult work, to lean into race, identity, equity, and teambuilding, Norka shared this powerful example of what is possible when trust is developed, and norms are set for Heartleading to occur in the workplace.

"Psychological safety is the product of centering our shared humanity, being anti-racist and anti-oppressive, affirming one another by valuing our assets, and ensuring spaces are trauma free- all important principles of equity. When we experience psychological safety we are free to be our authentic selves. When we are safe, we can thrive as creative, caring innovators, communicators, and problem solvers collectively while valuing our diverse perspectives. Equity work requires diverse perspectives in order to ensure all students are achieving their goals and aspirations with joy. Learning happens through doing, doing the work. Learning begins through relational trust that develops within the

community. We intentionally strive for psychologically safe spaces as a foundation for disrupting oppressive systems. Our team's professional learning always begins with a potluck where our team comes together to socialize and share a meal and joy. Then we move into a community builder where everyone engages in structured discourse about a topic that is both personal and related to the work and learning. Some topics we have discussed include; 1) Share a time when you felt you belonged and why. 2) Share a time when you took a test. How did you feel before, during and after? 3) Share something difficult you did this year that you feel most proud of, either personal or professional. Throughout the year, each team within our office presented their work and how it aligned to the principles of equity-centered, trauma-informed education. The intention was for each team to learn from one another and to understand how we are collectively working toward an ecosystem of social justice. At the end of the year, a member of the team stood up and said, 'I have worked in this office for many years. I have never learned and changed as much as I have this year. At the beginning of the year, I was so nervous about presenting. I was shaking and barely able to speak. But our topics were so important, and you made me feel so comfortable and interested in what I do to contribute. I feel like for the first time, people know what I do, that I matter, and that my work serving with children is important. And now I can stand up and speak to all of you with confidence and comfort. We have improved our service with students and families so much. Thank you.'"

The learning progression Norka was involved in creating with her team around this critical work, as well as the voice data testimony, speaks to her depth of spirit, commitment to scholarship and transparency, and her ability to be grounded in vulnerability. My previous outreach work with Norka taught me that she is incredibly knowledgeable in equity, diversity, and anti-racism approaches to supporting school communities and that her unique background and origin allow her to empathetically create very personal, authentic relationships with the families she serves in the school system.

"Authenticity, honesty, and trust are the foundation of love; an aspect of love is the action we take to reflect, improve, and humbly acknowledge mistakes of our own as well as guiding others to gracefully grow and improve."

Another example of Norka's leadership impact is built upon her advocacy and collaboration with multiple stakeholders and willingness to steward vulnerable populations.

"Our deep systems equity work is also found in the collaboration with our international office engaging with the math curriculum office. Most children in the world take integrated mathematics courses in secondary schools. There are only two states and one county in the United States that offer integrated mathematics, so converting these courses to the state-required courses of Algebra 1, Geometry, and Algebra 2 requires a deep analysis of mathematical standards to ensure children's academic identities are acknowledged and honored as the assets they truly are. (Norka and the teams were able to identify Math placement discrepancies built upon preconceived notions of these populations.) We now know that once someone has learned something, they don't need to learn it again in another language. When the integrated math courses were analyzed from countries all over the world, we revealed that most children in the world actually take Algebra 1 in 8th grade, Geometry in grade 9, and Algebra 2 in grade 10. We disrupted an inher-

ited, systematically racist math placement process with 'know better, do better.' Now international children have their mathematical identities acknowledged, are programmed into the next course they need, and teachers are receiving the professional learning they need to teach all children mathematics without putting children back in learning they have already done. Access is an extremely important aspect of equity that requires collaboration, valued diverse perspectives, and competent educators who know how to teach at grade level standards in culturally affirming ways for all children."

A wife and mother, Norka is the extremely proud mother of three adult sons in the fields of medicine, science, and communications. Norka is a Nationally Board Certified specialist in English as a New Language with two master's degrees and administrative certification. She also serves on the Board of the University of Maryland's College of Education Alumni Network. A lover of art museums and travel, Norka and her husband, Réal, enjoy adventuring locally and abroad.

"It's important to our communities that we all experience a stimulating, inspiring, and caring educational experience. When that happens, that's love."

Dr. Joshua Fine, Principal

"In the end, it's all about the love."

Josh grew up in a small town on the eastern shore of Maryland where he learned the importance of community and equity firsthand. Small towns come with the privilege of an extended family full of neighbors, friends, and mentors but can also lack the exposure and inclusion a young, in-the-closet, gay child craves.

"Leading from a place of love lives in my gay youth and early adulthood. I often felt embarrassed or shy to express my life experiences in public organizations. I feared that my differences would be judged or misunderstood. I kept them away from my professional life thinking that they would only cause harm or trouble if mentioned. My experiences help me normalize the many different lives I come into contact with and appreciate the importance of the work I do."

After high school, Josh left home in Salisbury, MD to attend American University in Washington, D.C., and it was there, in the nation's capital, where he fell in love with urban education. During this time Josh discovered that education was the greatest civil rights challenge of our time. After college, Josh began his teaching career in Montgomery County, MD as a social studies and English for Speakers of Other Languages (ESOL) teacher where he spent each day connecting with students and identifying innovative ways to connect kids to their educational experience.

"A Heartleader focuses on the feelings of those in their organization and their overall wellness rather than just the practical needs of the moment. We can attend to the collective emotional state of our staff and school by timing our initiatives well, intervening with wellness programs, and most importantly, just listen."

Josh is deeply committed to anti-racism and equity work in partnership with his colleagues and community. His scholarship has led him to earn a Master's Degree in Urban Education Policy from Brown University and a Doctorate in Educational Leadership from the University of Maryland Eastern Shore. Through his leadership and focus on caring, sustainable relationships, Josh advocates for all children needing access to a caring community, as well as adults who unconditionally support them with love and a world-class education.

Over the last few years, the academic and behavior intervention data in Josh's school positively reflected the leadership moves he has made, proving that creative, intentional teamwork around a shared vision can move mountains.

"I have connected educational equity and anti-racism to literacy. Literacy has been used throughout our country's history to marginalize certain groups of our population and continues to be a barrier to opportunity. Disproportionately, students of color and students living below the poverty line struggle to leave our schools as literate which will greatly affect their ability to fulfill their potential in school and work. At our school, we used resources to ensure our entire staff could support instruction that is based in the science of reading. This action has led to improved outcomes for emerging multilingual learners, Latino students, African American students, as well as proficiency rates overall."

"During the pandemic, we noticed that food security was a growing concern in our school community. During this period of time, we discussed different options with our community including establishing a pantry or creating a partnership with a community organization. After having a community conversation about not only our need but the desire *to have a solution, we honored each member of our community's dignity. We worked with our PTA and the local church to establish a bi-weekly grocery distribution that can be sustainable. Our grocery delivery has occurred every two weeks consecutively and without interruption for the last 2.5 years."*

A beloved principal with a warmth, charisma, and sense of humor that instantly endears others to him, Josh is continuously seeking out opportunities to close instructional gaps, partner with his community, and collaborate with internal and external stakeholders to address equity work. A leader who is admired and well-respected in the community, Josh is a true advocate for authenticity and love as transformative tools in the work of educators.

"Love comes into play in the work I do because it's the child that needs someone to love them as they struggle or thrive. The parent that trusts you enough to cry out for help. The staff member you've coached to a stronger place. Most importantly, the hustle and bustle of a school building filled with potential, home, and energy."

We've examined traits shared by leaders over years of conversation and observed practice and experienced the profiles of four, diverse Heartleaders.

> I'd love to hear stories about the Heartleaders in your life. Email the stories to me at Heartleaderlove@gmail.com. With their permission, we can feature them in my Heartleader social media.

Now, let's look at leadership in terms of when it is ineffective, when it is unsafe, and when it fails.

"Schools require sound decision making to reach successful outcomes... if school employees in positions of authority base their decisions on personal gain and subjective opportunistic outcomes that district is in trouble of failing and failing fast...if your staff is not well, it diminishes the thought and planning process. Emotionally sick staff members give birth to sick, toxic school environments. Emotional maturity is critical to the success of education environments."

-Dr. Kanteasa Rowell
District Administrator K-12 Specialized Instructional Services
Providence Public School Department, Providence, RI

Over the years, I have curated the voices of those I serve including students, parents, bus drivers, paraeducators, and more. The feedback documented in the following graphic is only an overview, but all of these have been demonstrated in school communities.

Figure 12

When Leaders Fail

When Leaders Fail

Behaviors That Harm Students

Lack of visibility in the building

Imbalanced application of behavioral interventions

Confrontational with children

Lack the ability to act from a place of empathy and compassion

Do not keep their word

Compromising children = risking their safety & success

Behaviors That Harm Staff

Fail to follow through

Fail to model expectations

Do not provide actionable, authentic feedback

Demonstrate a pattern of shaming staff

Work only in black and white, demonstrate inflexibility

Compromising staff = psychologically unsafe

Behaviors That Harm Families

Lack visibility at school events

Fail to consistently communicate

Fail to solicit and use parent voices

Inability to act with cultural competence & sensitivity

Inability to build sustainable relationships

Marginalizing parents = loss of partnership

HEARTBEATS

Heartleading encourages the leader in every one of us to reflect on the statements below.

- You must understand yourself--your origin--to authentically, empathetically lead others. Where have you come from? Where are you going?
- Successful educational leaders in any type of role and with any task know that success relies on a collaborative approach to solutions and implementation.
- Leaders are only as strong as the experts they surround themselves with.
- Risks and mistakes are a true part of the growth process when changing outdated plans, protocols, and policies.
- There is nothing passive about leadership work. It moves from an equity foothold, and is lensed through an anti-racist framework. It is an active state of being, and always includes the voices of all races, ethnicities, cultures, religions, and sexual orientation.
- No matter what path you choose, when you keep kids, families, and communities as the priority, you are on the right path.

Epilogue

The Further Adventures of a Heartleader...Unmasked

I've always wanted to find my place in the world, and in many ways, I've always struggled with that. It doesn't make me any better or different than any one of thousands of others who have been on that journey, but I guess what I am trying to say is that we're all on some kind of adventure, some kind of journey, and it's okay that this book, these words, find you wherever you are in that. It is incredible to meet you right now at this moment, and I want to lean into every bit of it with you.

That self-conscious, hyper-emotional, and very vulnerable part of me, part Super-Grover and part wanna-be Indiana Jones, is constantly making long-distance mental phone calls to that little boy of 3, 7, and 14, who is still with me, acting like his emotional GPS to find a way through everything. I am guessing that through reexamining your own stories, you are also trying to figure it all out, giving yourself grace and love, and trying to find a way through. It might be trauma. It might be the call to service. It might be the day to day, but here we are. Educators in this day and age, with all the hats worn are doing their best to build a way through. This work we are engaged in is very rewarding but incredibly difficult. Whether this book ends up on your shelf, your front seat, or at a training with colleagues, I'm glad we could share in this work together.

Preparing for my role each day and the work before me, I inventory my home and school balance, my personal healing, self-care, and professional development. I envision a mountain stacked with ledges of risks and some immense summit tucked up there within the clouds, a little like the ancient temple of legend hidden from the child version of myself, scaling the cabinet, reaching beyond the bathroom sink.

I've often witnessed that when you are climbing towards a goal, someone or something always seems to put a question into your path with a "Are you sure you should do this?" or the warning, "Whatever you do don't look down!" I understand those types of things better now; inexperience, fear, or lack of trust in yourself and your choices makes you want to listen to that doubt or respond to the need to look down. I understand more clearly because (1) I've gotten a lot healthier through my personal trauma work, and (2) I invest in myself, in cultivating my sense of self, and have finally matured into a better version of what I continue to want in my life. As a husband, father, and teacher, I feel like I stumble or fail a lot. In those moments I am continually climbing towards goals I set for myself, seeking footholds, places to get my grip just right, body pressed against the face of that proverbial mountain. It is precarious, terrifying really, and I don't want to make a move that will have me fall, but I climb.

It is hard to start, to place yourself–whole body, mind, and spirit–onto that mountain of yours. Just kicking off the first few steps is enough to make you catch your breath, but that's just it though, right? You breathe, you fill yourself with the gift of the experience, what you are *able* to do with your ascent. I wonder where your mountain will find you, and I wish for you a life-changing climb full of everything you need and a breathtaking summit.

The story of me has never been linear, and the parts, although fragmented and jumbled, are pulled together to define this boy, this man, this origin. I know I'll always live and love in this way appreciating everything lost and all the beautiful things gained; I'm the only me I can be. I realize in our collective storytelling that we, too, are now connected in looking with hope at those precious pieces we all carry. Somewhere between the sunrise and sunset, we'll all find one another up in the mountains reaching, climbing, walking along those paths.

My Hope For You

I hope for each of you the same thing I have hoped for myself, my wife, my six children, and my students: a chance. A chance to become the best version of ourselves; the most honest, patient, loving human beings we can be in this world. May your lives and your future storytelling be filled with love. In the end, it's about the origins and all about the love.

"Everyone wants to know more about love. We want to know what it means to love, what we can do in our everyday lives to love and be loved... we still hope that love will prevail. We still believe in love's promise."

-Bell Hooks

When you make your choice, *choose love.*

I'll see you in the schools and neighborhoods my friends. You'll know me when you see me. I'm the one with open arms, heart on my sleeve, ready to welcome you home.

Love Lives Here Crisis Support Resources

Rainn.org (Rape, Abuse, Incest National Network)
- National Sexual Assault Hotline: online chat available at website above.
- Telephone hotline: 800-656-HOPE (4673)
- DoD Safe Helpline: a service for members of the U.S. military and their families, operated by RAINN for the Department of Defense
- Telephone hotline: 877-995-5247

https://www.nimh.nih.gov/health/find-help (National Institute of Mental Health)
- Dial : 9-8-8 (Suicide and Crisis)

Acknowledgements

So many people have loved me to bringing this book into life–from stage to screen, conference room to classroom. Thank you to so many stand-up humans who challenged me and helped me. I am grateful to all of my educator brothers and sisters who contributed to this book, as well as all of my students and their families over all these years. Thank you Brad Weinstein, John Wick, Alaina Clark-Weinstein, Amanda Fox, Heather Brown, and the TeacherGoals team for believing in my work. Additional gratitude and love to my colleagues everywhere I have served, as well as Phyllis Fagell, Dr. Sarah Sirgo, and Desmond Mackall. A tremendous debt of thanks to a visionary, artist, and lifelong friend, Joe Mallek. Love always to my two mentors: Dr. Tony Leach, a father figure, a beloved friend, one of those who saved me and filled my life with music, theater, and above all, love and infinite joy, and Dr. Maravene "Mar" Loeschke-- so much of me is because of you. I love you, and I'll see you onstage once again, finding one another on our marks, there in the footlights. For Sesame Street, the Muppets, and all my heroes along the journey–comics, stage, and screen. To my parents and family for their acceptance and support of this kid who always marched–danced really–to his own Broadway beat in 4/4 time, love you all and thank you for your grace and patience.

About the Author

Matthew is a husband and father; these relationships have re-formed the foundation of his life. A Maryland native, he has served in education for over twenty-six years as a theater, musical theater dance, English, and special education teacher. He holds a B.A. in Theatre (Towson University), M.A. in Teaching, M.Ed in Educational Leadership (University of Notre Dame of Maryland), and is currently a PhD student at Bowie State University in Educational Leadership with a focus in Trauma-Responsive Teaching and Leading. Along the climb, Matthew was a police recruit and medic for the fire department and has worked in theater, television, and film as an actor, singer, dancer, director, and choreographer. An Emmy and Cine Golden Eagle- winning writer/director for his educational short film, 'BusSTOP,' on the bullying crisis, Matthew has also published numerous national articles, and writes, speaks, and provides trainings on trauma-responsive teaching and leading, designing trauma-sensitive spaces, social-emotional interventions, and school-family partnerships through TeacherGoals. You can find Matthew and his wife Kristi, a therapist and herself a former teacher, wandering the wilds, climbing those mountains, and crossing fallen logs with their children on any given day. They carry lots of snacks and water bottles for adventures, and perhaps a mask and cape tucked in the back pocket, just in case.

References

Aguilar, E. (2018). Onward—cultivating emotional resiliency in educators.p. 149.

Allen, K. (2022). The power of relationships in schools: growing and nurturing student belonging. *Psychology Today.* https://www.psychologytoday.com/us/blog/sense-belonging/202201/the-power-relationships-in-schools

Asquith, M. S. (2023). The impact of secondary traumatic stress, compassion fatigue, compassion satisfaction and burnout on public K-12 teachers [ProQuest Information & Learning]. *In Dissertation Abstracts International Section A: Humanities and Social Sciences.* Vol. 84, (4A). paragraph 6.

Brown, B. (2021). *Atlas of the heart.* pp. 170-17, 184.

Brown, B. (2018). *Dare to lead: brave work, tough conversations, whole hearts.*

Bryk, A., & Schneider, B. (2002). *Trust in schools: A core resource for improvement.* (as referenced in Garcia et. al, 2016, p.6)

Chapman, G. (1992). *The five love languages.*

Chopra, C. N. (2014). *New pathways for partnerships: An exploration of how partnering with students affects teachers and schooling.* (Unpublished doctoral dissertation. University of Washington). ProQuest Dissertations and Theses Global.

Chugtai, A. (2022). Trust propensity and job performance: The mediating role of psychological safety and affective commitment. *Current Psychology: A Journal for Diverse Perspectives on Diverse Psychological Issues.* Vol. 41, (10). pp. 6934–6944.DOI: 10.1007/s12144-020-01157-6.

Cipriano, C., Brackett, M. (2020). How to support teachers emotional needs right now. *Greater Good Magazine.* https://greatergood.berkeley.edu/article/item/how_to_support_teachers_emotional_needs_right_now

Compassion Prison Project. (2023). *Childhood trauma statistics: How common are childhood adverse experiences?* https://compassionprisonproject.org/childhood-trauma-statistics/

Courson, L. (2021). *Supporting teachers' social and emotional needs to improve teacher stress.* (Doctoral dissertation. Trevecca Nazarene University). ProQuest Dissertations and Theses Global. p.12.

Cook-Sather, A. (2020). Student voice across contexts: fostering student agency in today's schools. *Theory Into Practice,* 59 (2), pp.182-191.

Craig, S. (2008). Reaching and teaching children who hurt: strategies for your classroom. p.87, 90.

Curran, L. (2013). 101 Trauma-informed interventions: activities, exercise, and assignments to move the client and therapy forward.

Dweck, C. (2015). "Carol dweck revisits the 'growth mindset." *Education Week.* https://www.studentachievement.org/wp-content/uploads/Carol-Dweck-Revisits-the-Growth-Mindset.pdf

Eisenberger, N. (2012). The Neural bases of social pain: evidence for shared representations with physical pain. *Psychosomatic Medicine.* 74, (2). paragraphs 12, 18.

Epstein, J. L., & Salinas, K. C. (2004). Partnering with families and communities. *Educational Leadership,* 61, (8), pp. 12–18.

Fagell, P. (2017). Career confidential: Should teachers attend students' after-school events *KAPPAN.* https://kappanonline.org/should-teachers-attend/

Finkelhor, D., Ormrod, R. K., & Turner, H. A. (2007). Polyvictimization and trauma in a national longitudinal cohort. Development and psychopathology, Vol. 19 (1), pp. 149-166.

Freire, P. (1970). *Pedagogy of the oppressed.* pp.89, 90.

Garcia, M., Frunzi, K., Dean, C., Flores, N., Miller, K. (2016). Toolkit of Resources for Engaging Families and the Community as Partners in Education Part 3: Building trusting relationships with families and the community through effective communication. *United States Department of Education.* p. 6 https://files.eric.ed.gov/fulltext/ED569112.pdf

Gay, G. (2002). Preparing for culturally responsive teaching. *Journal of Teacher Education,* (53). pp.106-116.

Graham-Clay, S. (2005). Communicating with Parents: Strategies for Teachers. *The School Community Journal.* Vol.15 (1), p.126 https://files.eric.ed.gov/fulltext/EJ794819.pdf

Gyatso, Tenzin.(2023). Compassion and the individual. *His holiness the 14th dalai lama of tibet.* paragraph 4. https://www.dalailama.com/messages/compassion-and-human-values/compassion

Hafen, C., Ruzek, E., Gregory, A., Allen, J., Mikami, A. (2015). Focusing on teacher–student interactions eliminates the negative impact of students' disruptive behavior on teacher perceptions. International *Journal of Behavioral Development.* Vol. 30 (5).https://doi.org/10.1177/0165025415579455

Hammond, Z. (2014). *Culturally responsive teaching and the brain.* pp. 39, 40-41, 77.

Henderson, A., Mapp, K., Johnson, V., Davies, D. (2007). *Beyond the bake sale: the essential guide to family-school partnerships.* pp. 56, 62.

Hooks, B. (2000). All about love. p.xxviii

Itzchakov, G., Weinstein, N., Vinokur, E., Yomtovian, A. (2022). Communicating for workplace connection: a longitudinal study of the outcomes of listening training on teachers' autonomy, psychological safety, and relational climate. *Psychology in the Schools.* Vol, 60 (4).https://doi-org.proxy-bs.researchport.umd.edu/10.1002/pits.22835

Karandashev, V. (2015). A cultural perspective on romantic love. *International Association for Cross Cultural Psychology.* pp. 3-21. https://scholarworks.gvsu.edu/cgi/viewcontent.cgi?article=1135&context=orpc

Khalifa, M. (2018). *Culturally responsive school leadership.* pp. 103, 175, 192.

Kim, S., Crooks, C., Bax, K., Shokoohi, M. (2021). Impact of Trauma-Informed Training and Mindfulness-Based Social–Emotional Learning Program on Teacher Attitudes and Burnout: A Mixed-Methods Study. *School Mental Health.* Vol. 13. paragraph 3. https://doi.org/10.1007/s12310-020-09406-6

Leaver, E. (2020). Racial Equity in Your PTO or PTA: What Are You Doing? *PTO Today.* paragraph 5. https://www.ptotoday.com/pto-today-articles/article/9047-racial-equity-in-your-pto-or-pta-what-are-you-doing

Leech, J. (2020). 7 science-based health benefits of drinking enough water. *Healthline.* https://www.healthline.com/nutrition/7-health-benefits-of-water

L'Heureux Lewis-McCoy, R. (2014). *Inequality in the promised land: race, resources and suburban schooling.* p.119.

Mason, C., Rivers-Murphy, M., Jackson, Y. (2020). *Mindful school communities: the five cs of nurturing heart centered learning. p. 59.*

Maclean, L., & Law, J. (2022). Supporting primary school students' mental health needs: teachers' perceptions of roles, barriers, and abilities. *Psychology in the Schools.* Vol. 59, (11). paragraph 7, section 1.

Mehrabian, A. (1971). Silent Messages.

Merriam-Webster. (n.d.). Aperture. In *Merriam-Webster.com dictionary.* Retrieved June 16, 2022, from https://www.merriam-webster.com/dictionary/aperture

Merriam-Webster. (n.d.). Homeostasis. In *Merriam-Webster.com dictionary.* Retrieved July, 2021, from https://www.merriam-webster.com/dictionary/braggadocio

Merriam-Webster. (n.d.). In Loco Parentis. In *Merriam-Webster.com dictionary.* Retrieved July, 2021, from https://www.merriam-webster.com/dictionary/in%20loco%20parentis

Nikon USA. (2023). What is aperture? Understanding maximum aperture. https://www.nikonusa.com/en/learn-and-explore/a/tips-and-techniques/understanding-maximum-aperture.html

Messina, N. P. (2023). An experimental study of the effectiveness of a trauma-specific intervention for incarcerated men. *Journal of Interpersonal Violence,* Vol. 38 (3–4), pp. 3088–3112. https://doi.org/10.1177/08862605221104526

Perry, B. (2002). Neurodevelopmental impact of violence in childhood. In D.H. Schetsky & E.P. Benedek (Eds.) *Principles and practice of child and adolescent forensic psychiatry.* pp.191-203.

Perry, B & Szalavitz, M. (2017). The boy who was raised as a dog: what traumatized children can teach us about loss, love, and healing. pp. 258, 262.

Pollock, M. (2017). Schooltalk: rethinking what we say about and to students every day. p.59.

Rego, S., Fader, S. (2021). *The CBT workbook for mental health: evidence-based exercises to transform negative thoughts and manage your well-being.* pp. 7-11, 61-62.

Rodolfo, K. (2020). "What is homeostasis?" *Scientific American.* https://www.scientificamerican.com/article/what-is-homeostasis/#. paragraph 1.

Sadowski, M. (2016). More Than a Safe Space: How Schools Can Enable LGBTQ Students to Thrive. *American Educator.* p.6 https://files.eric.ed.gov/fulltext/EJ1123878.pdf

Schwartz, R. (2021). *No bad parts: healing trauma & restoring wholeness with the internal family systems model.* p. 186.

Schwartz, R., Olds, J. (2015). Love and the brain. https://hms.harvard.edu/news-events/publications-archive/brain/love-brain

Shirai, M., Toshi, T. (2019). Why is pain associated with sadness? Sadness is represented by specific physical pain through verbal knowledge. Vol. 14 (5). paragraph 1. https://journals.plos.org/plosone/article?id=10.1371/journal.pone.021633

Safir, S., Dugan, J. (2021) Street Data: A Next Generation Model for Equity, Pedagogy, and School Transformation. p.89.

Schneider, B. (2003). Trust in schools: a core resource for school reform. *Educational Leadership.* Vol.60 (6). https://www.ascd.org/el/articles/trust-in-schools-a-core-resource-for-school-reform

Serani, D. (2021). Re-Entry Anxiety in the Pandemic Aftermath. *Medpage Today.* https://www.medpagetoday.com/publichealthpolicy/generalprofessionalissues/91911

Shakeel, S., Khan, M., Khan, R., Muijtaba, B. (2021). Linking personality traits, self-efficacy and burnout of teachers in public schools: does school climate play a moderating role? p.20

Shevrin Venet, A. (2021). Equity-Centered Trauma Informed Education. pp. 35, 36, 85, 115, 128, 153.

Taylor, R. (2022). Love in action. *Hope: A lifestyle magazine.* www.hopeforwomenmang.com/hope-for-women-magazine/2022/1/31/love-in-action

Tomlinson, C. (2003). Fulfilling the Promise of the Differentiated Classroom: Strategies and Tools for Responsive Teaching. ASCD.

Tudor, K. (2022). Parents' perspective on the relationship of school climate and parental involvement: a phenomenological study. ProQuest Dissertations & Theses Global. p.16 https://www.proquest.com/dissertations-theses/parents-perspective-on-relationship-school/docview/2550464562/se-2

USCB. (2020). United states census bureau: 2020 census data. https://www.census.gov/data.html

USDE. (2023). United states department of education. Every student succeeds act (ESSA). Title 1, Part A. https://www2.ed.gov/programs/titleiparta/index.html

Van der Kolk, B.A. (2015) The Body Keeps the Score: brain, mind, and body in the healing of trauma. p. 98.

Williams, R. (2008). Cultural Safety what does it mean for our work practice? *Australian and New Zealand Journal of Public Health* 23(2). p. 213.

Wolpert, S. (2013). UCLA neuroscientist's book explains why social connection is as important as food and shelter. *UCLA Newsroom,* paragraph 3. https://newsroom.ucla.edu/releases/we-are-hard-wired-to-be-social-248746

Yale Center for Emotional Intelligence. (2013). RULER. Retrieved from http://ei.yale.edu/ruler/ruler-overview

More From

The Science of Reading in Action
By Malia Holowell

This is not just a book. It's a teaching movement! With 67 % of U.S. kids not proficient in reading, according to 2022 data, the status quo isn't working.

This book tackles the main obstacles: training, tools and support offering:
- Evidence-based insights on teaching, reading, dispelling social media myths
- Solutions for common challenges facing struggling readers
- Ready-to-use activities and strategies that simplify brain-friendly reading instruction
- A method to help students memorize words 10x faster than with flashcards
- Techniques to ensure no student falls behind

Written by Malia Hollowell, a certified educator and Stanford alum, this book is your all-in-one guide for making reading instruction effective and engaging.

The AI Classroom
By Dan Fitzpatrick, Amanda Fox, and Brad Weinstein

Are you an educator looking to stay ahead in the ever-changing world of education? Look no further than *The AI Classroom*, the ultimate guide for navigating the complexities of AI in education.

In *The AI Classroom* you will find:
- PREP and EDIT prompting frameworks
- 40+ prompts for educators
- 20+ AI tools to aide UDL guidelines
- 30+ AI tools educators can use NOW
- AI educational policy templates

Teaching In Sync
By Erica N. Terry and Dr. Lynea Laws

Teaching In Sync is a comprehensive guide to co-teaching success, covering everything from building a strong relationship with your co-teacher to utilizing AI for co-planning and incorporating technology for progress monitoring. With research-backed advice and a touch of NSYNC inspiration, this book will help you hit all the right notes in co-teaching.

Unlock the power of co-teaching with:
- 20+ downloadable resources
- Time-saving strategies to efficiently co-plan & progress monitor
- 50+ assistive and instructional technology resources
- 15+ AI prompts designed for co-teachers
- *In Sync* co-teaching framework

Children's Books

Peter O'Meter
By Tricia Fuglestad

Peter O'Meter is an interactive book that explores the emotional journey of a young robot named Peter. With an upgraded eMotion panel that needs calibration, readers can help Peter identify his feelings as he navigates his retro-futuristic world. This book offers interactivity and augmented reality to enhance the reading experience, allowing readers to interact with a 3D Peter, make decisions, and communicate their advice. Augmented reality animations bring the illustrations to life, creating an emotive and moving narrative.

Monsters Have Manners
By Jeff Kubiak

Monsters Have Manners is a charming children's book by Jeff Kubiak that teaches the importance of kindness and manners through the adventures of River and his monster friends. With augmented reality coloring pages, it offers an interactive reading experience for children aged 3 to 8. The story follows River and his love for monsters, despite their poor manners, until one night when the monsters visit River and everything changes.

Markertown
By Amanda Fox

Markertown is a children's story about a glitter marker who loses her cap and meets a group of repurposed markers on her journey to find it. The story encourages kindness and friendship, and highlights the importance of upcycling and embracing one's inner sparkle. With vibrant pages and interactive augmented reality coloring pages, Markertown is a great gift for children, teachers, and anyone who loves stories like *The Day the Crayons Quit* and *Not Just a Scribble*.

Upcoming Titles

Blueprint for Inclusion
By Rebekah Poe

Discover the essential guide to inclusive education in *Blueprint for Inclusion*. This concise, practical book offers educators research-backed strategies to support all students effectively, especially those with IEPs. Learn to navigate legal frameworks, foster collaborative teamwork, and create supportive classroom environments through actionable insights and real-world case studies.

Empower your teaching journey with strategies and wisdom that make inclusive education not just a goal but a reality.

Body and Brain Brilliance
By Dr. Lori Desautels

Discover the transformative power of *Body and Brain Brilliance*. Navigate through today's unprecedented stress with essential neuro-educational tools. Empower adults and children to cultivate emotional resilience and social connection, fostering classrooms where everyone feels seen, heard, and understood.

Dive in, and embark on a journey of healing and comprehensive well-being.

Unlocking SEL: The Blueprint to Social and Emotional Learning
By Lana Penley

Unlocking SEL by Lana Penley offers a transformative blueprint for education, seamlessly integrating Social and Emotional Learning (SEL) into classrooms. This guide explores essential strategies and real-life applications designed to cultivate mindfulness and foster a caring community. Dive into this invaluable resource for a journey that elevates the well-being of students and educators, ultimately creating a ripple effect of positive change in our educational landscape.

189

Printed in Great Britain
by Amazon